THE KEY ISSUES LECTURE SERIES
is made possible through a grant from
International Telephone and Telegraph Corporation

Multinational Corporations, Trade and the Dollar in the Seventies

Edited by
Jules Backman and Ernest Bloch

With a Foreword by
Harold S. Geneen

New York: New York University Press 1974

Copyright © 1974 by New York University
Library of Congress Catalog Card Number: 74-77713
ISBN: 8147-0977-X (Clothbound Edition)
ISBN: 0-8147-0978-8 (Paperback Edition)
Manufactured in the United States of America

Preface

Abraham L. Gitlow

Dean
School of Business and Public Administration
New York University

It is a great pleasure to introduce the second volume to grow out of the Key Issues Lecture Series of the College of Business and Public Administration, New York University, which was made possible by a grant from the International Telephone and Telegraph Corporation.

The current series focused on some of the crucial problems and challenges we face in our international economic relations now and during the remainder of the decade. As in the earlier series, we were privileged to bring to these issues the minds of some of the nation's most knowledgeable and respected economists, from the faculties of New York University, Harvard, and MIT. I have no doubt that the papers by Professors Jules Backman, Arnold W. Sametz, Raymond Vernon, and Charles F. Kindleberger will be well read and widely discussed. In fact their analyses have already been widely reported in leading newspapers and journals. Hopefully, this volume will provide a more permanent record of their thoughts, and will thereby enable an even larger audience to study and comment on them.

I would be remiss indeed if I did not express appreciation to Professors Jules Backman and Ernest Bloch who were instrumental in arranging the series, to my administrative assistants, Mrs. Patricia Matthias, for her handling of publication details, and Mrs. Virginia Moress, for her handling of the physical arrangements for the lectures, to the several other members of my office staff who saw to it that everything went smoothly, to Mrs. Catherine Ferfoglia who helped prepare the volume for publication, and to Mr. Malcolm Johnson and Mr. Robert Bull of the NYU Press, who saw to it that this volume appeared in a timely and attractive manner.

February 1974

Contents

Foreword

Harold S. Geneen

Chairman and Chief Executive Officer
International Telephone and Telegraph Corporation

The theme "Business Problems of the Seventies" has struck a responsive chord with those of us at ITT. As a multinational company with corporate responsibilities in some ninety countries around the world, we are vitally concerned—perhaps more than most—with expanding the fund of research and knowledge regarding the impact and future course of the problems we face today.

We are particularly pleased that sponsoring the Key Issues Lecture Series once again gives us the outstanding leadership of Dr. Jules Backman, Research Professor of Economics here at NYU. Dr. Backman was instrumental in organizing the first series, which has already generated a tremendous amount of favorable comment in both the academic and business communities. More than twelve hundred persons attended the series of eight lectures in the spring of 1973.

A volume of those lectures, edited by Dr. Backman, is now available under the title *Business Problems of the Seventies,* Volume I.

But I think Dr. Backman would agree, the most gratifying accomplishment of the series to date is the fact that it has stimulated a great deal of thought and discussion on the complex issues affecting the function of business in modern society.

Big business has been the target of some criticism lately, and there may be more to come. The learning experience, as the society of mankind continues to expand and prosper, will be fraught with missteps, miscues, and accusations from skeptics that the corporate citizen isn't living up to his social responsibilities.

Our objective is to encourage the critical reexamination of traditional economic theory in light of newly developed technology and heightened environmental considerations; and then translate the resulting analysis and dialogue into a usable format. The futures of the corporate and individual citizen alike are interlocked and totally dependent on the free exchange of information and the formulation of economic policy completely free of biased or outdated thinking. That's the reasoning behind our commitment to the Key Issues Lecture Series, and we are grateful for the leadership and support provided by NYU.

ONE

International Economic Problems

Jules Backman

Research Professor of Economics
New York University
and
Ernest Bloch

C. W. Gerstenberg
Professor of Finance
New York University

Against a background of currency floats, yen and D-mark revaluations, dollar devaluations, significant changes in trade balance, oil import crises, and enormous international flows of speculative and hot money, many national policy proposals represent retreads of the worst of neomercantilism. Some observers seem to have concluded that the international economy is in such disarray that it is heading for disaster. Such a view, which appears to our contributors to be misguided, has led to ill-advised policy prescriptions directed toward insulation of specific problem areas from these pressures. Such approaches are based on erroneous and partial diagnoses of the international problem and do not provide solutions for the economic problems they propose to solve.

The present problems faced by the world economy stem in part from the successful—yes, successful—emergence and rapid growth of international economic activity out of the Bretton Woods system of international monetary and trade arrangements. It should be recalled that the Bretton Woods and the follow-up agreements were designed to avoid the reemergence of the internecine economic warfare among nation states, warfare that had prolonged the Great Depression of the thirties. Up to a point, the postwar system did succeed and contributed to the restoration of a war-devastated Europe and Japan. But the process of subsequent rapid growth brought with it new problems. For example, the rigid foreign exchange relationships established in the post-World War II period could not withstand the new dynamic pressures, and as a result major changes have had to be made.

CHANGES IN POLICY PROBLEMS

The period since the end of World War II has embraced three distinct phases. The first lasted about a decade; it can be dated from the end of the war (or the beginning of the Marshall plan in 1948) to the advent of dollar convertibility of Europe's currencies (1958). This was a period of "dollar shortage" for the world's major economies. During this period, wartime scarcities outside the United States were gradually eased while foreign exchange controls were used to economize scarce dollar holdings. As foreign economies recovered, an increasing supply of goods and services became available for export, and U.S. foreign investments began to rise. Toward the end of the 1950s the flow of dollars abroad rose sharply, thus overcoming the shortage.

During the second period—lasting roughly from 1958 to 1971—the rapid recovery of Europe and Japan combined with sharply rising U.S. investment abroad resulted in a shift from a "dollar shortage" to a "dollar surplus." The dollar, as an international currency, provided the vehicle for a rapidly expanding international money market which led quite naturally to the development of a substantial international capital market. As a by-product of these developments, the U.S. balance of payments moved to a deficit, and as a result, the United States introduced exchange control policies to manage these deficits. There is considerable evidence that these control devices changed little more than the institutional aspects of the deficit; some evidence cited below indicates that the controls did not reduce significantly their magnitude.

The third period, which could conveniently be dated from the U.S. control measures of August 1971, has been characterized by increasingly realistic governmental policies in the United States to deal more directly with a dollar exchange rate that had moved progressively out of line with other currencies. In turn, this has led to two dollar devaluations as well as to experiments with currency floats by some of our trading partners. The foregoing does not really differ from Professor Kindleberger's analysis; it only distinguishes between the dollar yesterday and the day before yesterday (when there was still a dollar shortage).

CHANGES IN INTERNATIONAL FINANCIAL MARKETS

As the dollar moved increasingly toward serving as an international money and capital market in the 1960s, its exchange rate was stabilized to some extent by an ingenious but progressively less effective "ad-hoccery" of intergovernmental and intercentral bank arrangements. The notions that fixed foreign exchange rates were the central supporting arch of the international economy and that the fixed dollar rate was its keystone were being undermined by unanticipated side effects of the policy mechanisms that we now discuss.

Consider the fact that in the 1960s profound changes took place in the private sector of the world economy and were reflected in the growth of the multinational corporations (MNCs). The internationalization of financial markets for short- and long-term financing was essential for growth of MNCs. But this integration of the financial surface of the world economy required still another ingredient to become effective, namely, a substantial change in attitude toward growth and competition by the U.S. commercial banking industry. That industry, in effect, was a somnolent giant during the 1940s and most of the 1950s while recovering from the trauma of the Great Depression. But when it bestirred itself in the 1960s, it moved at home and abroad. In the United States, for example, banks began to compete much more aggressively for interest-bearing deposit liabilities so that by year-end 1967 time deposits exceeded demand deposits.

On the foreign scene, U.S. commercial banks experienced what can only be called an explosion of activity abroad in the 1960s. As Table 1-1 indicates, at year-end 1960, eight U.S. banks owned a branch network aggregating some 131 branches. By 1965, the number of U.S. banks with foreign branches had risen to 13, and their

Table 1-1

INTERNATIONAL ACTIVITIES OF U.S.
COMMERCIAL BANKS, SELECTED YEAR-
ENDS, 1960–1972
(operating data in billions of dollars)

	1960	1965	1968	1970	1972
A. *Branch Network* *					
Number of U.S. banks	8	13	26	79	108
Number of foreign branches	131	211	375	536	627
B. *Foreign Operations*					
U.S. credit to foreigners †	4.2	9.7	9.2	9.7	13.4
Assets of overseas branches ‡	3.5	9.1	23.0	52.6	90.2
Total foreign assets	7.7	18.8	32.2	62.3	103.6
C. *Memo Account*					
Assets, all insured U.S. banks	255.7	374.1	498.1	572.7	732.5
(%) Foreign assets/total assets		3.01	5.03	6.46	10.88	14.14

* Actual number of banks and branches.
† Includes foreign credits of U.S.-domiciled branches of foreign banks.
‡ Including interbank balances.
Source: A. F. Brimmer, "American International Banking," mimeo, Federal Reserve Board, April 2, 1973, table 1, and *Federal Reserve Bulletin,* various issues.

branch network aggregated 211 units abroad. From that year, the growth rate accelerated, so that at year-end 1972 some 108 (mostly) large U.S. commercial banks owned 627 branches abroad.

A glance at the magnitude and growth of foreign operations of these banks and their branches is even more instructive. Again, through 1965, foreign loan activity grew fairly rapidly, albeit from small beginnings, and reached a figure of total foreign credit and assets of not quite $19 billion. But then the system took off. Looking only at assets of foreign branches, these more than doubled in the three-year period 1965 to 1968, more than doubled once again in the *two-year* period 1968 to 1970, and almost doubled again in the last two years. Indeed, as the last row in the table indicates, foreign assets of U.S. banks have risen from a level just sufficient to provide worldwide service bureaus for a handful of banks to one-seventh of total U.S. bank assets. By this writing, most large U.S. banks are large multinational corporations, deriving a large share of profits from foreign operations.

The foregoing, while interesting and helpful in sketching an outline of one important set of MNCs (e.g. international banks) that will *not* be treated separately in this volume, can also serve as a useful example of how attempts by the United States to impose a number of exchange control devices (discussed below by Professor Kindleberger) led eventually to avoidance of those devices by both nonfinancial and financial MNCs. Consider, for example, the Voluntary Foreign Credit Restraint program, instituted in early 1965 to cut down on foreign lending by U.S. banks. This program led to the above-mentioned surge of bank branches and branch lending abroad. Table 1-1 indicates how restraints on direct lending to foreigners was followed by an explosion of branch lending. In effect, these foreign branches did the loan business abroad, frequently with U.S. multinationals, that the U.S. Department of Commerce did *not* wish to see done at home because of increasing balance-of-payments deficits. Beyond this, the availability of dollar loans at foreign branches had another unanticipated result: in periods of tight money and credit crunch in the United States, the home offices of international banks borrowed funds from their branches to offset, to some degree, monetary pressures at home.[1] As a result, interest rates in international money markets began to converge.

As these new financial circuits were being set up it did not take

long for new financial market arrangements to become institution-
alized. What are known as the Euro-dollar and Euro-currency markets got their start in the late 1950s and early 1960s. Growth was
slow until the mid-1960s, reaching a level of dollar and nondollar
liabilities of about $15 billion in 1965.[2] Within the next seven years,
however, these "offshore" deposits multiplied nearly nine times,
reaching $132 billion by year-end 1972.

A Euro-bond market also began to operate.[3] Both the Voluntary
Credit Restraint Program of 1965 (which limited direct lending by
U.S. financial institutions abroad) and its successor, the Mandatory
Control Program (1968), contributed to the development and growth
of the offshore bond markets. Controls over foreign investment were
ended early in 1974. Table 1-2 indicates that both U.S. and non-U.S.
companies, as well as other high-quality borrowers abroad, raised
large amounts of funds in the international bond markets.[4] Indeed
during the 1968–1972 period, flotations were on a scale larger than
that of any other single corporate bond market outside of the United
States.

The increasing capacity of international money and bond markets
to accommodate high-quality (that is, mostly large and multinational)
borrowers in the 1960s was fed by dollar flows. The development of
international financial markets presented for many countries an

Table 1-2

BORROWERS ON INTERNATIONAL BOND
MARKETS, 1968–1972
(in millions of dollars)

	1968	1969	1970	1971	1972
Bonds * issued by:					
U.S. companies	2235	1228	796	1298	2207
Non-U.S. companies	659	945	1148	1331	2104
Other †	1814	1810	1400	2551	4084
Totals	4708	3983	3344	5180	8395

* Sum of Eurobonds and foreign bonds.
† Includes state enterprises, governments, and international organizations.
Source: Morgan Guaranty, *World Financial Markets,* various issues.

"outside" competition with respect to credit availability and interest rates. As Table 1-3 indicates, even such sluggish rates as those on corporate bonds tended, through the nexus of that growing international bond market, to be subject to a new type of homogenization. Whereas the average of interest rates on major foreign capital markets was some 160 and 120 basis points higher than U.S. long-term corporate bonds in 1966, the deviation of that average from U.S. yields was subsequently reduced to the neighborhood of about one-half of a percentage point as foreign borrowings rose. Likewise, since 1966, the international bonds (e.g. Euro-dollar bonds and other international bonds) that served as alternative sources of funds for many U.S. MNC borrowers abroad held close to those on U.S. bonds in all but the credit-crunch year of 1969.

Against this background of well-established international money and capital markets, Professor Kindleberger sees the "dollar tomorrow" as an international currency whose role has declined from star performer to that of supporting actor. At the same time, his play is now without a star; it may well consist of six or more currencies in search of a numéraire. One somehow feels that special drawing rights (SDRs) are not mature enough for a starring role and that gold is a star whose day is long past—although reviews of occasional guest appearances still make the front page.

Dr. Kindleberger's point that the system will continue to evolve in ways not now foreseeable is well taken. No one foresaw the growth of the international financial markets that are such a prominent feature of the scene today. Indeed, the current rate of activity of MNCs would be unthinkable without those markets as we now know them. And this brings us to Professor Kindleberger's last point, namely, that the scale of international markets is importantly a function of the depth, breadth, and resiliency of the U.S. capital market at home. Perhaps the supporting role in the play is the most important one after all.

In sum, the group of MNCs called international banks (with U.S. and foreign parent units) and the investment banking units active in international markets, have provided a true financial innovation, namely, an international money and capital market. The dollar served as the vehicle currency for these markets. As its exchange rate came under pressure, it was but natural for policy makers to consider ways of dealing with each of the "new" problems of the dollar. It

Table 1-3

INTERNATIONAL COMPARISONS OF LONG-TERM BOND YIELDS, 1966–1972
(yields in percentage per annum)

	1966 Jan.	1966 Dec.	1967 Dec.	1968 Dec.	1969 Dec.	1970 Dec.	1971 Dec.	1972 Dec.
U.S. domestic corporate bonds	4.95	5.70	6.74	7.04	8.95	7.90	7.30	7.33
International bonds *	6.33	6.38	6.87	7.25	8.13	8.08	7.77	7.62
Other domestic corporate bonds:								
Canada	6.03	6.83	7.59	8.18	9.29	8.83	8.24	8.15
Japan	7.82	7.54	8.57	8.66	9.07	9.20	7.38	6.75
Belgium	5.68	6.05	6.05	5.92	6.96	6.92	6.12	7.74
France	7.25	7.71	7.52	7.76	8.71	8.83	8.69	8.30
Germany	7.50	7.80	6.95	6.43	7.60	7.77	7.59	8.58
Italy	6.63	6.71	7.15	7.12	8.51	9.74	8.46	8.67
Netherlands	6.44	7.12	6.71	6.98	8.54	7.88	7.91	7.81
Switzerland	4.60	5.19	5.11	5.13	5.58	6.09	5.42	5.47
United Kingdom	7.27	7.63	7.97	9.16	10.70	10.84	9.19	10.40
Average of all non-U.S. issues	6.56	6.90	7.05	7.26	8.31	8.42	7.68	7.95
Deviation of average from U.S. yield	+1.61	+1.20	+0.31	+0.22	−0.64	+0.52	+0.38	+0.62

* U.S. companies, dollar-denominated issues.
Source: Morgan Guaranty Trust Company of New York, *World Financial Markets*, various issues.

was noted earlier that partial policy treatments of financial symptoms by one sort of exchange control or another only deflected the problem into a different direction. But in the 1970s, a worsening of the U.S. trade balance once again led to demands for protectionism.

A POLICY RETREAD: PROTECTIONISM IS THE WRONG ROAD

In a world that easily had become used to the benefits of economic affluence, it has been easy to forget—or to ignore—the economic policies that helped make it possible. In the quarter-century after World War II the world economy experienced the longest period and largest expansion of prosperity in its history. It is easy to ignore the lesson taught by the Great Depression that preceded World War II, namely, that it is in the power of government policies to stop growth, generate unemployment, and promote the tragedy of waste. It is no accident that postwar growth was accompanied by generally successful efforts to ease barriers to international trade, to contribute to optimization of outputs through international specialization, and to open up international financial markets to facilitate the flow of international goods and services.

Table 1-4 suggests quite clearly that a close association exists between periods of the large export growth rates and the rising quantity of world production (as a proxy for the sum of real national incomes). During the postwar period as a whole, all but one of the subperiods shown indicate substantially more rapid growth rates in real world exports (or imports) than in world output. As a result, it is not surprising that a new set of problems has arisen, that inflation rather than unemployment is now the major invisible policy export of industrialized countries.

In that context, claims for tariff or quota protection appear to be irrational. But such proposals were given added impetus by the fact that the United States, in 1971, experienced a deficit on merchandise trade for the first time in this century. And when the U.S. trade balance worsened further in 1972, and was followed by a second de-

Table 1-4

COMPARISON OF QUANTUM INDEXES OF
WORLD PRODUCTION AND WORLD EXPORTS,
SELECTED YEARS 1948–1972

Years	World Production	World Exports	Annual Rates of Increase *	
	(1963 = 100)		Production	Exports
			(in percentages)	
1948	45	39	—	—
1953	62	55	7.6	8.2
1958	70	71	2.9	5.8
1963	100	100	8.6	8.2
1968	137	152	7.4	10.4
1972	165	212	5.1	9.9

* Compound annual rates of growth between years listed.
Source: *U.N. Bulletin of Statistics* (United Nations, New York), September 1973.

valuation of the dollar in 1973, the stage was set for proposals for a policy regression to the bad old days of protectionism.

However, the U.S. balance of trade (as well as the overall balance of payments) has sharply improved during the latter part of 1973. These changes can be interpreted as a case of economic variables lagging—as one might expect—behind earlier policy moves. The Burke-Hartke bill and Nixon trade proposals were under active consideration at the very time that U.S. trade and capital movements already were responding to prior policy measures, and in a period following the presumably learned lessons of the postwar experience noted above. The proposals for a new protectionism represent a clear-cut case of cultural rather than economic lag.

Chapter 3, which deals with protectionism, can serve as an antidote to what might be called the inappropriate conditioned-reflex approach to setting economic policy. And events have shown that such an educational effort is urgently required.

A NEW POLICY QUANDARY: MULTINATIONAL FIRMS IN AN ENVIRONMENT OF NATIONAL CONTROLS

Despite the growth of an extensive literature, policy makers within national states still lack the concepts on which to build policies for MNCs. The problem of developing an appropriate intellectual foundation for rational decisions by authority, national or international, is more than a case of cultural lag or perceptual myopia. The MNC (whether financial or nonfinancial) is an innovation in the profoundest sense. It requires new understanding as a prerequisite for deciding how it should be supervised, how investors should evaluate its performance, and how competitors should adjust to it.

The problem of perception may be illustrated by the contrasting reactions to the development of MNCs in Europe and in the United States. In Europe, emphasis has been given to the invasion of American MNCs, and in some countries it has become a critical political issue. In the United States, on the other hand, emphasis has been directed to the impacts on the balance of payments, the balance of trade, and the impact on employment in this country when MNCs with U.S. origins establish plants overseas. The concern by the AFL-CIO that the employment effects have been adverse led to the introduction of the foreign-investment control elements of the Burke-Hartke bill which were designed to restrict imports and to make investments overseas unattractive by major increases in taxes on overseas profits (see Chapter 3).

There are many noneconomic areas which are affected by MNCs. It is several of these areas that Professor Vernon covers in Chapter 4. MNCs operate in different countries and are subject to a bewildering variety of local laws and local practices. Foreign-owned companies may be treated differently from those locally owned.

The need for analysis of MNC purposes and functions also enters the area of *internal* corporate management. In Professor Vernon's words: "To what extent do nationals in the home office continue to identify with their home government, and to what extent do local managers abroad identify with the nation from which they derive their nationality?"

Economists generally are concerned with the efficiency of various economic institutions and deal with the extent to which they contribute to a nation's economic well-being. Too little of the available analyses subject MNC to this test. However, Professor Vernon suggests that the meager data available "lend support to the generalization that the multinational enterprise generally performs efficiently as compared with the available alternatives." Nevertheless, it is not clear how the benefits of this greater efficiency are or should be distributed.

In recent years, the issue of social responsibility of business has become important.[5] In this country, it has taken various forms including improvement in the environment, fair employment practices, help to minority groups in establishing new businesses, slum clearance, etc. But there are sharp differences of opinion as to how far and how rapidly progress should be made in these areas. Conflict between environmentalists and those seeking to solve the energy problem has taken place in many areas including the Alaska pipeline, the building of nuclear power plants, offshore drilling for oil, strip mining (coal), the speed with which auto emission standards should be imposed, etc.

Not all countries are moving at the same speed in the areas of social responsibility or agree upon what social objectives shall be. How shall MNCs react to this situation? Will they seek to build new plants in countries which do *not* enforce strict antipollution standards? How shall they adjust to varying standards established in different jurisdictions? To changes in such standards? The problems of MNCs are necessarily more complex than those of strictly national companies. As a result, they may *not* be able to achieve much movement toward the goals of social responsibility unless international standards are developed.

Professor Vernon suggests that while it is now difficult to improve the social performance of MNCs, it should be possible to develop their social accountability. To achieve this goal requires greater cooperation between governments and possibly the establishment of intergovernmental agencies. Among the areas identified for such action are taxation, policies toward competition and monopoly, subsidy policy, and labor relations. The adoption of policies dealing with these areas has been extremely difficult within a country; the coordination of policies between countries would appear to face almost insuperable barriers. Yet, the growing proportion of both national and international activity accounted for by MNCs indicates that attempts will be made to apply some degree of international regulation to their activities.

Many important questions remain to be resolved. How shall such international regulation be established? Through the United Nations? Or by the establishment of new intergovernment agencies? Can tax policies be coordinated through international agreements? What standards of accountability shall be promulgated and by whom? What controls, if any, should be imposed over the international transfer of funds by MNCs in order to contribute to stability of foreign exchange markets? Can the widely varying attitudes among countries toward problems such as pollution be harmonized so that meaningful international standards can be set up? Will the developing countries be willing to accept any regulation of MNCs so long as they are seeking and bidding for much needed capital investment from these companies?

Clearly, the agenda of problems is long, and progress toward their solution must be slow if we are to avoid losing the benefits of MNC activities because of the hasty adoption of unwise policies. Professor Vernon describes in detail the problem areas and notes some tentative solutions. However, as he concedes, these are first steps. Much remains to be done.

THE FOREIGN MULTINATIONAL IN THE UNITED STATES

The extensive discussions of the role of the multinational companies have focused on the magnitude and effects of the investment by U.S. MNCs overseas.[6] The multinational company is not solely an American phenomenon. Many companies headquartered outside of the United States also have been making direct foreign investments in the United States. In effect, to achieve their size many of the world's largest companies have become multinational in scale and operate in leading countries throughout the world, including the United States. An examination of the 300 largest foreign industrial companies listed in the *Fortune* tabulation for 1972 shows that 105 of these firms each had more than $1 billion in sales and 109 more had between $500 and $1 billion.[7]

Foreign MNCs have been increasing their participation in the American economy both by the establishment of new plants (e.g. two Japanese companies announced plans to build electric furnace steel mills) [8] and by the acquisition of American companies (e.g. the bid for control of Texas Gulf, Inc., by the Canadian Development Corp. and the acquisition of Stouffer by Nestlé, a Swiss company).[9] The sharp decline in American stock prices in the last few years and recent devaluations of the dollar have brought equity prices of many American companies to bargain levels for foreigners. Foreign companies have not been averse to picking up these values because many companies are selling at very low price-earnings ratios.

Accordingly, in 1973 there was an increasing number of announcements of foreign take-overs of American companies. In some instances foreign companies have outbid American companies. For example, Brown & Williamson, a subsidiary of a British company, outbid Loews for control of Gimbels in mid-1973.

On an overall basis, the U.S. Department of Commerce reports that total foreign direct investment in the United States [10] was $14.4 billion at the end of 1972.[11]

In the years 1962 to 1971, the total value of direct foreign investments in the United States increased by about $6.4 billion of which "$2.6 billion came from net capital inflows while nearly $3.8 billion was reinvested earnings." [12] Between 1966 and 1970, the total investment increased by an average of about $800 million a year, or more than twice as rapidly as in the preceding four years. The inflow of net direct investments slowed down in 1971, as foreign firms began to anticipate a depreciation of the dollar, and then increased again in 1972.

What will be the effect on the American economy of an increase in direct investments by foreign MNCs? When new plants are established here, a new competitor enters the market and total output in this country is stimulated. If the foreign company transfers overseas know-how to its new plant in this country, new production techniques are introduced and in time will infiltrate throughout the industry. Conversely, know-how may also flow abroad to the benefit of all concerned.

According to Professor Sametz, the objectives of direct investment in the United States by foreign MNCs are quite different from those of their U.S. counterparts. Foreign MNCs enter the enormous U.S. market precisely because of *this market's size:* entry into the market improves the *scale economies* of the foreign firms whether their products are sold here or abroad. U.S.-based MNCs already enjoy that scale advantage, and their direct investments abroad are designed essentially to hold on to a share of a foreign market by avoiding tariff and other barriers. When foreign-based MNCs gain scale economies through direct investments in the United States they can compete on better terms with U.S.-based counterparts, not just in this country, but also at home, and most notably in third countries.[13]

Despite the above difference, it seems clear that many MNCs are beginning to look more and more alike, no matter where their original place of incorporation. As a result, many decisions by MNCs probably are made on the basis of *multicountry* criteria. This suggests that references to "countries of origin" or "majority ownership" may represent classifications that are declining in relevance.

Nevertheless, individual countries still control national boundaries and execute policies that will affect their own balance of payments. As "foreign" direct investment increases in the United States, the transfer of foreign funds to this country results in a demand for dollars and hence initially has a positive effect upon our international balance of payments. With the passage of time, this net positive effect will be reduced or modified and ultimately may become negative in individual instances, as the transfer of interest and dividends to the parent company overseas increases. Conversely, to the extent that a firm's growth in investment in the United States is financed by the reinvestment of the American subsidiary's cash flow, the "outflow effect" may not occur or be quite small.

Because the value of investments in this country by foreign MNCs is still small and reinvestment has been a relatively large part of the rise in value, public criticism has been fairly well muted. As the magnitude of these investments is increased and their characteristics change, public attitudes, too, may change. American companies may complain about the increasing competition because there may be some loss of sales to the local plants of foreign MNCs and/or from their foreign plants. Congressmen can be expected to make speeches to the effect that the American economy is being dominated by foreign companies, that we are at the mercy of their whims, that there is a "Défi Européen."

This brief review of some of the impacts of foreign MNCs in the United States suggests a number of questions which will become of increasing concern. To evaluate the emerging problem, better data are required concerning the magnitude of these investments and the impact on the industries which are most affected. To what extent will this trend become an important factor in our balance of payments? Although the impact is rather small at the present time, how soon will it become significant? To what extent will foreign companies operate in a manner which is traditional in the American economy in contrast to how they operate at home? For example, will Japanese companies treat their American labor force as having a permanent attachment to jobs, as is done to a large extent in Japan, or will they follow the American pattern of periodic contraction and expansion in employment as the economy fluctuates? To the extent that they follow the Japanese pattern, how will this affect labor practices of American companies or change the characteristics of collective bargaining demands? To what extent has the depreciation of the dollar accelerated the trend, and to what extent will more flexible exchange rate arrangements add a new characteristic to the world's investment cycles?

Are there differences in the motivations underlying overseas investments by U.S. MNCs and those which play a role in foreign MNC investments in the United States? To what extent are the quantitative and qualitative economic impacts of foreign MNCs in the United States similar to those of American MNCs overseas? These questions indicate that many research opportunities are available and that we need a considerably greater volume of data and analysis before the full impact of MNCs on the American and the rest of the world's economies can be determined.

SOME CONCLUSIONS

Perhaps the best way to visualize the present situation is to break with received conceptual attitudes and take a fresh look at the international economic structure. Consider, for example, that total U.S. direct investment abroad now stands in the neighborhood of $100 billion at book value, with a market value probably several times that amount. Consider further that annual sales of these foreign units are probably about $180 billion, or almost three times as large as U.S. exports. While there has been international preoccupation with the role of U.S. MNCs abroad, comparable companies have developed in Europe and Japan with the consequent new dimensions to international competition and the development of new factors affecting worldwide financial and trade flows. In addition, worldwide networks of U.S. and foreign banking systems are enthusiastically involved in facilitating these multinational transactions.

A realistic perception of the world economy suggests that many proposed policies designed to deal with the emerging system may reflect, at best, a cultural lag, or at worst xenophobia. Worse yet, these misconceptions carry in them the very dangers that the Bretton Woods system was designed to avoid, namely, threats to economic stability, to economic growth, and to worldwide levels of economic well-being.

The decade of the 1960s undoubtedly was a period of unusually rapid economic experimentation and innovation. The internationalization of industry, the competition offered abroad by the penetration of U.S. corporations, and the upsurge of new money markets, such as the Euro currency systems, represent major structural changes in the international economy, with powerful side effects for policy management of national economies.

To be sure, conflicts arose between countries, and within countries as change brought on new problems. And, indeed, a bird's-eye view of international negotiations to resolve nation-state conflicts in the 1970s suggests that high-level negotiators (such as central bankers, secretaries of the treasury present and past, and ministers of finance) represent forces of *national* interest. By and large, their freedom to negotiate is constrained by national or domestic interests that tend to lead to separation or segregation of national economies. Meanwhile, behind the scenes, the profit-oriented actions of business managers and bankers erode and break through national boundaries, develop multinational corporations and banking systems, and thereby generate pressures toward increasingly integrative financial forces.

And foreign central bankers have not been averse to using these Euro markets as substitutes for intervening in domestic money markets that are too thin. The fact that we are experiencing such phenomena as the increasing similarity of worldwide interest rates and worldwide pressures toward inflation suggests that these changes carry certain costs. International integration, like the best things in life, is not free.

There are, of course, many other important international economic problems and policies which are not covered in depth in this volume: the effects of higher prices and withholding of Arab oil, the multinational control of investments, international patent policy, the economic role of the developing countries, the impact of the population explosion, the emerging role in international trade of China and Russia, the rising expectations of people throughout the world, the shortages of raw materials and foods, foreign aid, etc. But we hope that the papers to follow will help in suggesting approaches to meet some of the major problems.

NOTES

1. In an attempt to hold down such borrowings, the Federal Reserve in October 1969 placed special reserve requirements against home-office Eurodollar financings.
2. For further discussion of these data see Bank for International Settlements, *Annual Report* (Basle: 1973), pp. 154–170. It may be noted that after the Euro-currency market reached substantial size it became a complete money market in the following way: Some European central banks engaged in open market operations in that market to influence *domestic* credit conditions because their own internal markets were insufficiently developed.
3. For the first useful discussion of the development of this type of intermediation see E. Despres, C. P. Kindleberger and W. S. Salant, "The Dollar and World Liquidity: A Minority View," *The Economist* (London), February 5, 1966.
4. Prior to 1968, borrowing volume was substantially less. Earlier data were as follows:

Year	Volume (millions)
1963	$ 553
1964	983
1965	1417
1966	1520
1967	2405

5. See Lee Loevinger, "Social Responsibility in a Democratic Society" in *Business Problems of the Seventies,* ed. Jules Backman (New York: New York University Press, 1973), chap. 9.
6. See, for example, *Implications of Multinational Firms For World Trade and Investment and For U.S. Trade and Labor* (Washington: U.S. Tariff Commission, February 1973).
7. *Fortune,* September 1973, pp. 204–207.
8. *The Wall Street Journal,* August 24, 1973, p. 12.
9. *Business Week,* July 7, 1973, p. 561.
10. "Foreign-owned U.S. firms include all U.S. firms in which a foreign person or organization holds 25% or more of the voting stock or an equivalent interest" (*Survey of Current Business,* February 1973, p. 29, n. 2).
11. *Survey of Current Business,* August 1973, p. 50.
12. *Survey of Current Business,* February 1973, p. 33.
13. This scale argument is an analog of the proposition noted above that Eurodollar money and capital markets are effective because the domestic U.S. financial markets are large and efficient.

TWO

The Dollar—Yesterday, Today, and Tomorrow

Charles P. Kindleberger

Ford Professor of Economics
Massachusetts Institute of Technology

INTRODUCTION

In this paper I propose to limit my discussion of the dollar to its international aspects. The related internal question of inflation is important, but in its technical dimensions lies outside my interest and competence. On the international side, moreover, narrow questions dealing with, say, the Euro-dollar market will be left out. Rather I shall deal with international money. "Yesterday" concerns the role of the dollar as international money up to about 1971. "Today" provides a comment on the period since the Smithsonian Agreement of December 1971, and especially the period of floating. "Tomorrow" will attempt to assess what international monetary standard will replace the dollar if its international monetary role is altered, as seems inevitable. When I chose the title of this lecture last summer I had hope, but little expectation, that the meeting of the International Monetary Fund at Nairobi would throw light on this last question.

It did not, and we are on our own. Before we get to this question, however, we need the usual running start of the economic historian. Let us turn then to yesterday.

YESTERDAY

For some considerable period in this century, to about 1971, the world functioned on the dollar standard. It is of no consequence for what follows what date one picks as the launching of the dollar as international money: World War I; the postwar loans; the 1934 change of the gold price; 1936, when the Tripartite Monetary Agreement provided the first recognition on the part of this country of responsibility for the international monetary system; or World War II, when this country furnished the world with bilateral assistance through Lend-Lease, GARIOA (Government and Relief in Occupied Areas), the British loan, Marshall Plan and Point IV, and took a leading role in international organizations such as UNRRA for relief and rehabilitation, the International Bank for "Reconstruction and Development" (World Bank), and the International Monetary Fund (IMF) for financing balance-of-payments deficits. Whenever it started, the dollar standard was in full operations in the 1950s and began to run down in the 1960s. Ostensibly a gold-exchange standard, the dollar standard had little use for gold in its early stages. Gold is a poor international money: produced in arbitrary amounts and at great expense, clumsy to ship and store, and necessarily converted before it can be spent, the gold standard inevitably tends to evolve into the gold-exchange standard, with exchange replacing gold in transactions, in balances, and in use. The gold standard evolved into the sterling standard in the nineteenth century, and into the dollar standard in the twentieth.

The difficulty with a gold-exchange standard, however, is that it is subject to Gresham's Law—that bad money drives good into hoarding. Triffin's original criticism of the gold-exchange standard that it failed to produce enough liquidity [1] was wide of the mark. Liquidity could readily be manufactured. Some countries converted some aid into reserves, rather than using it for real assets, and when the period of aid came to an end for Europe and Japan, reserves could be added to by international financial intermediation, i.e., borrowing long and lending short. Rueff recognized the threat of Gresham's Law and proposed to abandon the gold-exchange for the gold standard, requiring countries to limit their exchange reserves and convert them to gold.[2] This would have reduced the number of reserve assets from two to one. An alternative, realized in practice, was to limit conversions. France tried to discipline the United States through extensive gold conversions in 1965. This helped to precipitate the two-tier system of March 1968 which detached the world price in private markets from the price at which central banks were ostensibly prepared to trade gold. In reality, it meant that central banks no longer dealt in gold; who wants to sell even to a colleague at $35 what is traded in another market at $43 (as it was in those days)? When the National Bank of Belgium in August 1971 tried to convert its dollars to gold, the system broke down and convertibility became a relic of the past. The realities of the situation were recognized in November 1973 when central banks agreed that they were free to sell gold to the open market at any price at all. It remains completely ambiguous whether central banks are permitted to buy gold, or to value it on their balance sheets at a price above $42.

There are other ways to cope with Gresham's Law than to reduce the reserve assets of the international monetary system from two to one. The Posthuma plan for requiring central banks to hold gold and exchange in fixed proportions was a sort of symmetallism. Harrod, Gilbert, and others would have kept the value of gold in line with the dollar reserves by raising the gold price *pari passu* with the increase in the supply of dollars,[3] although this would probably have destroyed the myth of gold's intrinsic value. In the end, the instability of two reserve assets was tackled by adding a third, the Special Drawing Right (SDR), although the logic of the move is open to question. The problem was to prevent the continuous deterioration in the reserve ratio of the United States, as dollar liabilities to foreigners mounted and gold, when it was not declining, merely held its own. But politically it would have been impossible to create SDRs for the United States alone. In fact, it proved impossible to restrict their manufacture to financial centers, as the less developed countries (LDCs) insisted on a share of the goodies, despite their almost total lack of interest in liquidity as distinct from imports and real capital formation.

Suppose, however, that it had been possible to solve the instability question inherent in Gresham's Law. Would the dollar standard have worked then? The economics of the solution are relatively simple; the politics exceedingly difficult. The system would have worked if it had been highly asymmetric between the United States, which would serve as bank, and the rest of the world, which can be said to consist of "traders," depositors, borrowers, but not themselves bankers. Such an asymmetric system functioned passably well in the forty years before World War I when sterling was world money, and the Bank of England ran its monetary policy—occasionally with help from the Bank of France—on the basis of its international position.

Mundell has indicated the shape of an asymmetric system of this kind.[4] The United States has two targets and two instrumental variables: full employment and world price stability, world monetary policy and fiscal policy. Each other country in the system also has two targets and two instruments, but they differ from those of the United States in important respects. The targets are full employment, as in the United States, and balance-of-payments stability; the instrumental variables are fiscal policy and differences in the interest rate from world monetary policy as laid down in the United States, not necessarily by the United States since U.S. monetary policy could be determined with the participation of, or after consultation with, the rest of the world.

Notice that in this system the United States had to regulate its monetary policy in the general international interest, and not on the sole basis of domestic needs, and it must ignore its own balance of payments which is the residual of the balances of payments of the rest of the world. If the rest of the world wants continuously rising reserves in dollars and there is no device such as SDRs for the United States or a rising gold price while U.S. gold reserves were still ample, the United States balance of payments is continuously in deficit, export and import-competing industry are under some deflationary pressure from overvaluation, and there is danger of a run on the bank. For the system to function efficiently, it must be understood by the countries involved, there must be political tolerance for asymmetry, the United States must determine its monetary policy in the interest of world stability, and other countries must be forebearing in the amounts of additions to reserves they demand.

None of these conditions was met, and there was an unforeseen structural change which would have been disturbing even if the system had functioned smoothly. Both European countries, such as Germany, Italy and France, and the United States acted as if their money markets were not joined, and pursued independent monetary policies. The result was large-scale movements of funds, despite foreign-exchange controls, and via the Eurodollar market, in search of higher interest returns. The series of separate measures to disconnect money markets—the Interest Equalization Tax in 1963, Federal Reserve regulations and Gore amendment in 1964, Voluntary Credit Restraint Program in 1965, Mandatory Control Program in 1968— each was taken as if the particular movement of capital was alone responsible for the outflow, and in ignorance of the fact that money is fungible and will flow through one or another conduit in succession as only one source of outflow is attacked. Restraints on outflow from the United States were ineffective, and so were the devices such as the "Bardepot" in Germany [5] and the two-tier exchange system for commercial and financial francs in Belgium and France. Italy managed to control an outflow of capital by supporting its regulation by bodily searches of border crossers.

The structural change may be linked to the failure of understanding in monetary policy, but it is not clear how. Sometime in the spring of 1970, the current account in the United States balance of payments began to deteriorate sharply, especially against Japan, Canada, and Germany. The automotive agreement with Canada was a major contributing factor, as United States automobile companies rearranged their production schedules by shifting output to Canada, but one would expect the Canadian-United States balance of payments to adjust to this change over time. Much more significant was the change vis-à-vis Japan. It is sometimes ascribed to the poor articulation of business cycles: Japan finding herself in depression as business in the United States picked up; but the econometric evidence made clear it was much more than could be explained by the normal coefficients of income and price elasticities. My hypothesis, for what it is worth, is that economic growth in Japan has been speeding up and in the United States slowing down, rather like the Climacteric in Britain at the end of the nineteenth century when Germany was expanding rapidly in new industries and innovative capacity in Britain was lagging. The timing in the spring of 1970 was perhaps too concentrated to support a theory of such a long-drawn-out and evolutionary character, but some structural changes seem to have been in train, and of such strength that they have resisted—at least for a time—a 40 percent appreciation of the Japanese yen.[6] After a couple of years, when the Nixon Administration had been cool to the sloshing about of short-term funds in benign neglect of the problem of the dollar, Secretary of the Treasury Connolly reacted with resolution and in some views bloody-mindedness in forcing through the devaluation of the dollar in the late summer and fall of 1971 with the help of the import surtax.

There were a few technical features of the problem which might be mentioned, such as the creation of Eurodollars outside the United States as foreign central banks recycled to the Eurodollar market the dollars that their residents had borrowed at rates below those at home and converted to local currency to refinance domestic indebtedness or for investment in real assets. The forces that tended to reduce European interest rates to those in the United States thus also piled up new dollars to be borrowed. This effort was slowed down by agreement in June 1971 among the major central banks, but the lesser banks, such as those of the oil countries, felt no responsibility for the system and continued to deposit their dollars in London at higher interest rates rather than in New York at lower. In addition, the credit crunches of 1966 and again of 1969–70, with interest rates rising in the United States for domestic reasons, brought tightness to London as United States banks tumbled over themselves to acquire Eurodollars to add to their deficient reserves in the United States, although it was impossible to add to total dollars by such means—the process involving merely a passing of reserves from one bank to another—except to the extent that dollars were provided to the market in the final analysis by the Federal Reserve System.

By the fall of 1970, the crunch was over, and the Federal Reserve System embarked on a cheap-money policy *à outrance,* flat out. New dollars created, however, lowered interest rates briefly, stimulated capital outflows, and in company with the change in the current account, led to short speculation against the dollar. With three sources of pressure against the dollar, and especially the structural one, the Administration decided to break up the dollar standard as the basis of the international monetary system. The rest of the world did little to deter the change. In May 1971, the German finance minister deliberately provoked a crisis by suggesting that the Deutschemark was undervalued. Speculation produced the necessity for a revaluation upward. In August 1971 came the Belgian conversions, and the import surtax plus the end of convertibility and domestic price control (to which President Nixon, whispering "I will ne'er consent," consented). Four months later at the Smithsonian Institution, an agreement for the revaluation of the dollar was signed after arduous negotiations. The dollar standard was through.

TODAY

President Nixon hailed the Smithsonian Agreement as the greatest financial agreement in monetary history, thus perhaps being somewhat less than fair to the Genoa agreement, Tripartite Monetary Agreement, Bretton Woods, the Basel Agreement, and a dozen others. Other observers than President Nixon, however, thought that the trouble with the dollar was that it was overvalued, and that once this was corrected it would be possible to return to the status quo ante, or the scene of the crime, and resume the old international monetary system with a central role for the dollar. Gottfried Haberler, for example,[7] judged the prospects for the dollar favorable. The optimism seemed premature.

First, the current account of the balance of payments did not turn around despite a 9 percent depreciation of the dollar and an even larger decline against the yen and Deutschemark. Elasticity optimists who had expected small changes in the price of the dollar to spur exports and to restrain imports began to discover the J-curve, which suggests that things get worse before they get better, and econometric evidence which notes that the benefits of some depreciation are not fully harvested until five years have gone by. There was still no explanation of what happened to the economic relations between the United States and Japan, or why an adjustment of the exchange rate would not cure it, but it was judged necessary to settle down and wait.

In the second place, the funds that had been taken out of the United States were not returned after the exchange-rate adjustment, leaving a large and uncertain "overhang" of foreign central-bank holdings of dollars. Had asset holders and speculators been content to take their foreign-exchange profits, and to buy back the dollars sold earlier as they returned to the "natural" currency "habitat"—to borrow an expression from the money market for different maturities —the central banks could have sold off a sizeable portion of their dollar holdings for their own currencies. But there is a difference between a "depreciating" and a "depreciated" currency; speculators will sell the former and buy the latter. The Smithsonian adjustment was judged to be only the "first bite of the cherry." So asset holders and speculators were unwilling to "return home," and in the course of staying out of dollars a long time, some of them undoubtedly developed into emigrants, leaving that part of the overhang itself permanent.

Thirdly, the lesson about joined money markets requiring one interest rate and only one had not been learned. Cheap money in the United States in 1970 had finally brought down European money-market rates. However, in the summer of 1972 European central banks began to worry about inflation and to pull them up again. Previously the United States had made the moves, and, however reluctantly, Europe and Japan followed. This time the United States, embroiled in a political campaign and seeking booming prosperity, resisted the pull of European rates. It may have been thought that the new exchange rate was sufficient to isolate capital markets and to permit Europe, off the old dollar standard, to have independent monetary policies. Independence went in only one direction. Capitalists and speculators were willing to go short of dollars, and would sell dollars against European currencies and yen if interest rates were lower in the United States. It is unlikely that they would sell DMs, francs, and yen and buy dollars if rates were higher in the United States. In any event, this time the United States followed the European lead. By December 1972, the Federal Reserve System found it difficult to hold the interest rate down. Dollars generated were going abroad rather than driving down domestic rates, and with them went additional existing dollars to bid up rates in the United States. The Federal Reserve had forgotten, if it ever knew, that the classic advice of Walter Bagehot is to discount in a speculative crisis but to do so only at a penalty rate. Feeding speculation by pumping dollars into the system as they go abroad makes sense only if a country seeks to depreciate its currency positively—what used to be called a beggar-thy-neighbor policy in depression, but one which in a period of inflation can be regarded rather as hoisting oneself on one's own petard.

For a minute in the summer of 1972, it looked as though the United States administration was going to be both more adroit and more open about the dollar. This was when Arthur F. Burns (chairman of the Federal Reserve Board) at a Montreal conference of bankers in August attacked the policy of benign neglect for the dollar on the ground that the value of the dollar was an international and not merely a United States concern. This seemed to recognize the importance of exchange-rate stability to the world system. (To this critic, however, Mr. Burns lost all the credit for this wisdom, and more too, when in the spring of 1973 he insisted, against the evidence of interest rates rising in the United States into line with European, that monetary policy was going to be made not in Paris or Frankfurt but in Washington.)

Adroitness and openness do not seem, however, to go together in this administration. In January 1973, Phase II of price controls was ended before it had produced a real slowdown to inflation, and prices bounded up again. The money supply was rapidly expanded to support the business boom. Speculators joined the interest arbitrageurs, and in one week in February the Bundesbank, trying futilely and virtually alone to hold the exchange rate, bought $9 billion dollars, while the Federal Reserve Bank of New York supported its own currency to the extent of less than one-twenty-fifth of that amount, i.e., $330 millions. If this was open, it was not adroit; if it was adroit, and the administration actually was trying to devalue the dollar further, it was not open. The morality escapes me of permitting your allies to help you and then pulling the plug on them by aiding speculation they are trying to resist.

Then came the second devaluation of an additional 10 percent followed by floating, clean floating without intervention or management. Sitting as I do at some distance from the decision center in Washington, I am uncertain whether the cleanliness of the floating was ideological, with its origin in the Chicago school, which believes in the superiority of markets over the decisions of governments, or whether it was the result of inadvertence—a continuation of benign neglect. In any event, it is presumed that the decision to float clean was initially based on the view that the second devaluation had gotten the rate about right, and that the dollar was as likely to appreciate as to depreciate further. As it happened, more depreciation was in the cards. The upward surge of prices, aided by devaluation, discouraged speculators from covering, as did the enormous size of the overhang. In April and May 1973 came the Watergate scandal, which did not help. By July, it was decided that intervention might be called for to prevent destabilizing speculation from getting the bit in its teeth and running away. There is a Chicago school view that destabilizing speculation is impossible. Perhaps this is a response to the shift from horse-drawn vehicles to internal-combustion engines. The latter don't have a bit, nor any teeth into which it could get. But those of us who go back to the horse-and-buggy days are aware from the literature, even if each of us may not have seen a runaway horse, that destabilizing action can occur in horses.

On July 9 and 10, it was agreed that the Federal Reserve Bank of New York, which had been virtually sidelined up to that point, might manage the dollar, bringing to bear on the exchange market its "feel" for whether the dollar was oversold and technically strong because of the great volume of short positions being maintained at high rates of interest. By this time, it should be noted, the effort of the Federal Reserve Board in Washington to hold down interest rates had been thoroughly frustrated. Chairman Arthur Burns learned, or was at least exposed to, the lesson that United States interest-rate policy was made in Europe. Floating was now to be managed. The secretary of the treasury, the chairman of the Federal Reserve Board, and others allowed as how they thought the dollar was undervalued, and it did rise to some degree in the market in the summer of 1973. Overall, however, it had depreciated 40 percent against the yen, 39 percent against the Deutschemark and 22 percent against the French franc. The pound sterling, the Italian lira, and the Canadian dollar chose to depreciate against the strong currencies with the U.S. dollar. Since that time it has recovered substantially, largely as a result of the relatively greater blow dealt to the economies of Europe and Japan by the Arab oil boycott. It is not that the dollar has been strong: the franc, DM, guilder, and especially the lira, the yen, and sterling have been weak. But the U.S. dollar as international money was finished.

The dollar remains a medium of exchange and unit of account, but it is no longer in an international sense a store of value or a standard of deferred payment. The unit-of-account function is greatly damaged. People have to stop and think now when they are told that income per capita in Sweden is higher than in the United States. They should, to be sure, have been suspicious prior to the first devaluation at the Smithsonian, when the numbers showed that national income per capita was higher in the United States than in Sweden, or Australia, or New Zealand. The dollar was then a poor unit of account to the extent that it was overvalued, and in any event one should measure incomes in real terms, by such elaborate and ambiguous (because of the index-number problem) devices as that worked out by Gilbert and Kravis for the OECD [8] in the 1950s, in which the Swedish level of living is measured at U.S. prices, the U.S. level at Swedish prices, and the two somehow averaged. Before August 1971, however, the slippage in the accuracy of the dollar as a unit of account was slow and tolerable. Today, with an overall weighted 20 percent depreciation, there is no adequate measure of economic quantities which can be normalized in percentage terms. It is difficult to say that it is cheaper to produce a given article in one country or another for calculating comparative advantages. The dollar is still functioning as an international unit of account, but badly.

The dollar no longer serves as a store of value or standard of deferred payment. By the latter capacity, of course, is meant that it is not regularly used for contracts. Eurodollar bonds lost ground to securities denominated in other Euro currencies, such as the D-mark, and to composite units representing currency averages. Where the debtor or creditor has a choice of several currencies in which to pay or receive payment, the exchange risk is multiplied, since the debtor will pay in the cheapest, or the creditor demand receipt of the dearest. Averages are preferable. But they are more complex than using a single international money, and they do not eliminate the exchange risk. For some purposes, as, for example, where a resident of one country lends to a compatriot, there is no exchange risk to begin with —although risk of inflation—and the use of a currency average introduces an exchange risk to both. In the usual international loan, however, the averaging procedure moderates the risk of both debtor and creditor.

The reason that Eurodollar bonds did not lose out altogether, of course, is that exchange risks can be compensated by changes in interest yield.

Other contracts, for shoes, and ships and sealing wax, or more accurately, for ships, oil, gas, coffee, cocoa, nonferrous metals, airfares, and the like give rise to a variety of devices in the absence of an international money such as the dollar. In oil, five-year contracts are torn up each time the dollar alters in value. In June 1973, the Organization of Petroleum Exporting Countries (OPEC) reached a new agreement with the oil companies tying the price of crude oil to an eleven-currency index which triggers a change in price whenever the index moves more than 1 percent a month. In a region where politics dominate business, it did not last long. In tankships, some contracts are written in yen, which skews the exchange risk one way, some are adjusted afterward to take account of exchange-rate changes which unduly penalize buyer or seller. Norwegian charters are moving down from long to short charters. Post hoc adjustment is the way it seems to be done in nonferrous metals to achieve an equitable result. The cocoa agreement broke up altogether: reopened to take account of the gyrations in the yardstick, it was impossible to close it again. And the International Air Transport Association finds itself in virtually continuous session to agree on new air fare schedules. Sir Henry Maine, the great British jurist and historian, indicated that social evolution was a gradual process from status to contract, or in the words of Talcott Parsons, from diffuse relationships in society to specific, i.e., contractual. With the loss of the dollar as international money, the direction of movement is reversed, and runs from contractual to diffuse. It seems likely that the longer the system goes without a basis for clear contractual relations, the larger the opportunities for differences in view as to what is fair, and the more the difficulties.

The dollar is finished, at least temporarily, as an international store of value. As mentioned earlier, asset holders seem to have changed their habitat. Oil sheiks are leery of the dollar, apart from the political response to the Israeli-Arab war; international corporations, however much they may claim not to have been responsible for selling the dollar short, at least do not now buy it long when they accumulate foreign currencies. They seek advice from banks and foreign-exchange consultants, whose firms are springing up like mushrooms, as to what currencies to buy and sell and when, or they add more staff to the treasurer's office as they seek to provide for themselves privately the store-of-value function of international money which used to be furnished by the stability of the dollar.

The world monetary system proceeds on the basis of managed flexible exchange rates. It is agreed the system is unsatisfactory and in need of change, but there is little agreement how to go about changing it. The United States wants symmetry, by which it means pressure on the surplus as well as on the deficit country in the adjustment process and as wide a range of fluctuation for the dollar as for other currencies. More frequent currency adjustments and monetary reform tied to burden resharing in defense and to trade negotiations which adjust the protective agricultural policies of the European Economic Community. France, at the other extreme, wants stability of exchange rates first with no connections between money and trade or defense, and especially convertibility of the dollar into gold and SDRs. The less developed countries insist that the need for international monetary reform furnishes the occasion for providing foreign aid for developing nations, as seignorage from the issue of new money goes to them. At the Fund, which is the issuer of SDRs and the agent of international monetary reform, three vetos seem likely to inhibit action. The United States had a veto from the outset with a quota and therefore a voting share of 23 percent. The Common Market acquired one in the course of expansion of the separate national quotas and the extension of the Community to nine countries. The LDCs are normally each looking after itself, but on an issue like monetary reform, which offers the possibility of real assets for all, they are likely to hold up motion until they get paid off. But there is no consensus, and since the United States no longer has the desire or the capacity to provide leadership, the international monetary system is in anarchical disarray.

A number of countries have begun to use flexible exchange rates for internal stabilization rather than balance-of-payments adjustment. West Germany was an early leader in 1961, and lately in May 1971. More recently Australia, New Zealand, and, for a second time, the Netherlands have undertaken upward revaluations in the interest of dampening price inflation. The practice evokes echoes of the past. In 1930, Australia and New Zealand and Argentina started the wave of competitive currency depreciations, partly for balance-of-payments

reasons but also in an effort to fend off world deflation. The depreciation so undertaken was characterized as a beggar-thy-neighbor move
because it added to world deflation. Today, the converse holds, and
appreciation which is intended to ward off world inflation from a
country, adds to it. In 1931 to 1933, the United States and the gold
bloc were among the last to feel the concentration of world deflationary forces upon them. Today, the United States feels the effect of
world inflation through the rise of foreign-trade prices, as other
countries appreciate their currencies and the dollar depreciates.

TOMORROW

Tomorrow in the sense used in this paper is not likely to arrive
until quite a few more yesterdays have been piled up. The situation
as just indicated is one of no consensus, no leadership, and three
vetos. It has been agreed that exchange rates shall be fixed but ad-
justable. This sounds suspiciously like the Bretton Woods formula,
which all countries agree deserves to be consigned to the ash barrel.
The Common Market under French leadership insists on mandatory
convertibility, which used to be convertibility into gold under de
Gaulle, though faith in gold seems to be moderating under Pompi-
dou. The United States would like to see convertibility optional,
giving countries the opportunity to hold foreign exchange, by which
it means dollars. The British, lacking both gold and a currency in
recent demand, would like to shift over to a brand-new system in
which the SDR is the numéraire, the vehicle currency, the intervention currency—in short, international money; all parties are far from
agreeing how this should be done, even if they were able to agree
that it should be done, as they are not. Should SDRs be allowed to
be held by the public? What rate of interest should they bear? Is the
"link" really feasible, granting for the sake of argument that it is
equitable? Would an SDR system tend, like the gold standard, to
evolve into an SDR-exchange standard, with all the difficulties this
would pose for Gresham's Law? Would foreign exchange above max-
imum working balances have to be converted by central banks into
SDRs, or would convertibility be optional? If an important country

changed its exchange rate against SDRs, would other countries which traded with it be allowed or forbidden to make a parallel move?

Merely to list the questions is to indicate the difficulties in arriving at an agreed formula. I would propose that the effort be given up in favor of a piecemeal rather than an apocalyptic approach to the problem, proceeding as the way lies open, as my mother-in-law used to say, on a common-law instead of a constitutional, or perhaps one should say marriage-certificate, basis. But before I get to how I see the world monetary position evolving, let me make a point which is vital to our understanding of the dollar tomorrow.

The soothsayers find themselves awed by a portentous bit of balance-of-payments sooth, or truth, or reality, as they contemplate this country's prospective oil bill and its impact. The more naive of them extrapolate a rise in oil prices and volume to numbers such as imports of $25 billion a year, and become disheartened as they calculate that this will produce a deficit of $25 billion a year by some date not far away, such as 1985. Both the projection of oil imports and the analysis which converts imports into balance-of-payments deficit are unacceptable. It is true that oil imports have been rising rapidly in recent years in volume and price. To extrapolate this for twelve years into the future is to assume that the price system has failed to work. Higher prices bring substitutes. Exploration is proceeding rapidly outside the OPEC countries. Coal, atomic energy, oil shale, offshore drilling, Alaska pipelines, reductions in emission standards, control of speeds, and a host of other alternatives will be explored and put into operation before the dire predictions of the doom-sayers are realized. Their extrapolations are based on a microeconomic analytical fallacy.

And even if oil imports were to reach $25 billions annually, it is a macroeconomic fallacy to assume that this would increase the deficit by the same amount. This is not a partial-equilibrium, ceteris paribus question, like the price of World Series tickets in a stadium that holds only 50,000 spectators, but a general-equilibrium, mutatis-mutandis, changing-other-things-which-have-to-be-changed-type question, to offer you a mouth-filling substantive phrase as a modifier. Twenty-five billion dollars subtracted from our national income will cut down on other imports and release resources to add to exports and import-substitutes. In addition, in the oil-exporting countries, the $25 billion would increase national income and spill over into imports, or end up in savings and be invested abroad, perhaps in the United States. The analysis must trace the feedbacks through the entire system, not blithely assume that there are no feedbacks.

It could happen that the Persian Gulf countries sold oil to the United States and used the proceeds to buy imports from and invest in Europe and Japan. This makes tracing out the multilateral flows more complex: incomes rise in Europe and Japan and spill over into more imports from the United States or less exports. If the United States for structural reasons or because of the wrong exchange rate is not competitive with Europe and Japan, this cannot be ascribed to the original oil imports but to the structural change or the wrong exchange rate. I have no more time to devote to this compound fallacy of economic reason, but for those of you who have spent sleepless nights worrying about this issue as a long-run affair, I would advise relaxing, or if you like to stay awake, finding another problem.

Let me return to the international monetary system and the dollar. I predict that international monetary reform by governments will fail for the reasons stated. I believe that the system will evolve over time into a new shape in which it chooses some international money and the world uses it as a medium of exchange, unit of account, store of value, and standard of deferred payment. Governments propose; markets dispose. The Knapp view of money as the creation of the state was never persuasive. Money is what the market uses as money. And international money is what the market uses as international money. The real pressures are stronger than the theories of us ivory-tower economists and the ideologies of governments.

Few are any longer beguiled by gold as the French used to be, and few believe that the dollar, the Humpty Dumpty of tomorrow's financial scene can be put back together again by all the king's finance ministers and all his central bankers. Other national currencies such as the DM, the Swiss franc and the yen are shy and unexperienced as international money. Their officials try to keep foreign funds out, rather than to welcome them in. If you believe in the game which says if A, B, C, and D don't qualify, this makes E the natural candidate, we are left with the SDR as money. My logic, however, runs against acclamation by elimination. To evoke an old boxing remark about two poor fighters, neither man can win. Even if the SDR could get legislated by political means over the three vetos in the IMF, it would not succeed for technical reasons.

The gold standard evolved into the gold-exchange standard for reasons of efficiency. Gold was expensive to produce and to ship, cannot be spent without conversion, and needed to be assayed before conversion. The SDR escapes many of the physical drawbacks of gold. However, it suffers from the crucial inconvenience that it has to be converted into national money before it can be spent. There are, moreover, many issues as to how it would be used, whether it bears interest and how much, whether central banks obtaining foreign exchange are obliged to convert it to SDRs or may hold either asset (thus setting up again the possibilities of Gresham's Law), and especially whether SDRs can be held by the public. If the public cannot hold the SDR, it seems likely that the public will set up another national currency as its own international money to perform the functions of money. If international money is not provided to the public, the public will fix on a currency as international money. If it can hold SDRs it will want to be able to spend them, and with the SDR as international money the world may be bound even tighter together than it is now.

The question naturally arises whether the dollar will ever again serve as international money. Never is a long time, as children say, and I hesitate to suggest that it will never do so. But the conditions under which the dollar would come back into international use are so many and varied that it is unlikely that they will be achieved within a decade or two. This country must recover from its political malaise and get back some portion of its economic vitality. There must be willingness again to assert world economic leadership in Washington, and to assume an undue share of the burdens of running the world economy. This means maintaining an open market for distressed goods, countercyclical capital movements, rediscounting in a crisis, and policing a reasonable stable system of exchange rates. I see little evidence on any hand of a willingness to undertake these tasks in the country. Congress wants to pull the troops back and cut off foreign aid, labor is unwilling to permit imports; in a crisis we get help from others rather than struggle to meet our own problems. It takes two to tango, and even if we were prepared to lead, it is not clear that the other countries of the capitalist world would follow or even cooperate much.

There is one argument that I have heard only lately, after I had begun the draft of this lecture, and which I have not mulled about long enough to have an informed instinctive reaction. The thesis runs to the effect that the largest national money and capital market will dominate, and that means a comeback for the dollar. Two depreciations, a sharp decline and recovery, highly erratic monetary policy, worse exchange policy, and a series of political scandals count for less, in this view, than the fact that in no other money or capital market can a firm switch $10 million from thirty-day paper into ninety-day bills, commodities, bonds, or equities without affecting prices and yields. The availability of credit and narrow spreads are more important than the chaotic path of the exchange rate.

I respect this view, and I must confess that it may be right. My instinct, however, says it is wrong. My conclusion, therefore, is that the world and the dollar are in for an extended period of uncertainty. The United States will not assert leadership in the international monetary system. There is no other potential leader. The monetary system requires leadership. The conclusion then is that we all bumble along.

NOTES

1. Robert Triffin, *Gold and the Dollar Crisis* (New Haven: Yale University Press, 1960).
2. See, for example, Jacques Rueff and Fred Hirsch, "The Role and Rule of Gold: An Argument," *Essays in International Finance,* no. 47 (Princeton, June 1965).
3. See, for example, Milton Gilbert, "The Gold-Dollar System: Conditions of Equilibrium and the Price of New Gold," *Essays in International Finance,* no. 70 (Princeton, October 1968).
4. For a discussion of the "assignment problem," see the paper by that name by Egon Sohmen in *Monetary Problems in the International Economy*, ed. Robert A. Mundell and Alexander K. Swoboda (Chicago: University of Chicago Press, 1960), pp. 183–197, and especially the bibliographical note p. 183, including three papers by Mundell.
5. The "Bardepot" is a requirement that German banks receiving foreign

deposits hold special reserves against them at the Bundesbank. These can be as high as 100 percent.

6. See my "An American Economic Climacteric?" in *Challenge,* January–February 1974.
7. "Prospects for the Dollar Standard," *Lloyds Bank Review,* July 1972.
8. See M. Gilbert and Associates, *Comparative National Products and Price Levels: A Study of Western Europe and the United States* (Paris: Organization for Economic Cooperation and Development, 1958).

THREE

Protectionism Is the Wrong Road

Jules Backman

Research Professor of Economics
New York University

The total volume of foreign trade is affected by many factors other than tariffs and nontariff barriers. Changes in foreign exchange rates, controls over international capital flows, tax policies concerning overseas earnings, foreign aid, and other governmental policies have impacts on the levels of imports and exports. The close relationship between exchange rates and trade is highlighted in the conflict of opinion as to whether agreements on a new worldwide monetary system must precede or follow agreements dealing with tariffs and nontariff barriers. The two areas are so closely interrrelated, however, that ideally the solutions to both problems should be wrapped up in one package. At the minimum, every effort must be made to achieve progress simultaneously in both areas in the hope that the programs finally agreed upon will be made effective at the same time. In this paper, however, emphasis is given primarily to tariff and nontariff barriers.

During the past few years a considerable body of support has developed in the United States for various protectionist measures to limit foreign trade. Manifestations of this trend are found in the "voluntary" quotas for exports of textiles, steel, and other products to the United States negotiated with several foreign nations or foreign producers, import quotas imposed for oil and some dairy products, the unwillingness of Congress to approve some aspects of the Kennedy Round (e.g. the elimination of American Selling Price for some chemicals), and the extremely protectionist Burke-Hartke bill.

Before examining the reasons for the change in some attitudes in recent years, it is useful to review the actions taken to liberalize trade in the period since 1934 and their effect upon the volume of world trade. Since the shift in our trade balance has been a significant cause for concern, we must also examine the factors alleged to contribute to that development. Such an analysis indicates clearly that protectionism does not provide the answer.

TARIFF HISTORY

Throughout most of our history we have followed a high-tariff policy. The peak of protectionism was reached with the passage of the Smoot-Hawley Tariff Act of 1930. Almost every other major country retaliated with such measures as import quotas, exchange controls, and/or higher tariffs.

The passage of the Reciprocal Trade Agreements Act in 1934 marked a dramatic shift in our trade policy. The president was authorized to enter into agreements which reduced existing duties up to 50 percent. The reductions agreed to with any country were to be extended to other nations with which we had most-favored nation clauses.

The program was extended on several occasions and additional reductions were authorized in 1945, 1955, and 1958. The Trade Expansion Act of 1962 permitted the United States to bargain for further reductions of up to 50 percent of the prevailing levels for most tariffs and to negotiate with the European Economic Community for cuts of up to 100 percent.

As a result of this liberal trade policy, U.S. tariffs have been reduced significantly. Duties collected as a percentage of value of dutiable imports fell from an estimated 52.8 percent in 1930 to 7.0

percent in 1970.[1] This decline in the relative importance of tariffs reflected the price inflation, which increased the value of imports, as well as the reductions in rates.

WORLD TRADE GROWTH

The worldwide liberalization of tariffs and the dismantling of pre-war exchange controls after World War II was accompanied by an explosive growth in world trade. A few figures show the trends (see Table 3-1).

In 1972, free world exports were more than six and two-thirds times as large as in 1950, while U.S. exports were almost five times as large. These dollar totals are affected by the general price inflation in recent decades. However, physical volume also has increased sharply. For example, between 1955 and 1968, U.S. imports in real

Table 3-1

WORLD TRADE, 1950–1972

	Free World Exports	U.S. Exports	U.S. as Percentage of Free World
	(billions of dollars)		
1950	55.8	10.2	18.3
1955	83.4	14.4	17.3
1960	113.3	19.7	17.4
1965	165.4	26.4	16.0
1970	280.7	42.0	15.0
1971	314.9	42.8	13.6
1972	372.2	48.8	13.1

Sources: *Economic Report of the President,* January 1973 (Washington: 1973), p. 293; *Economic Indicators,* July 1973, p. 24; International Monetary Fund, *International Financial Statistics,* 1972 Supplement, pp. XII–XIII and July 1973, p. 36.

terms increased 1.6 times as much as real domestic output; real exports increased 1.4 times domestic output.[2] Familiar illustrations of large annual imports into the United States include more than fifteen million tons of iron and steel, more than one million automobiles, and millions of radios and television sets.

Many factors contributed to the growth in the volume of world trade, including the rising levels of living throughout the world, the dramatic expansions of the Japanese and German economies, the development of the Common Market, foreign aid programs, and the marked expansion of private international investments. Important facilitating factors were the sharp reductions in tariff barriers, the dismantling of the prewar currency restrictions by major trading nations, and the elimination of internal controls.[3]

The large rise in trade contributed to expanding gross national product with the accompanying increase in job opportunities and in living standards in many countries. A rise in world income and welfare has been associated with the rise in trade. A new wave of protectionism would result in serious disruptions to world trade with the accompanying adverse effects on output and employment. In this connection, the Tokyo meeting of GATT in September 1973 approved a declaration which tied together "the expansion and ever-greater liberalization of world trade and improvement in the standard of living and welfare of the people of the world." [4]

Factors Contributing to Protectionism

The strong movement toward protectionism has reflected several developments: (1) concern by the AFL-CIO over an alleged "export of jobs," (2) the shift in our trade balance from an export surplus to an import surplus, (3) the growth of the Common Market, and (4) the vigorous expansion of Japanese trade.

ALLEGED EXPORT OF JOBS

One of the main reasons for the concern about foreign trade has been the alleged "heavy export of jobs." The AFL-CIO has estimated that "the deterioration of the American position in international trade resulted in the net loss of about 900,000 *job opportunities* from 1966 to 1971. . . ." [Italics added] [5]

It should be noted that this estimate refers to the loss of "job opportunities," not to a reduction in the number of jobs. The AFL-CIO has cited fifteen industries in which allegedly "jobs were lost because of imports." For each of the industries listed, imports generally increased sharply between 1965 and 1971. Nevertheless, employment actually increased in nine of these industries (glass, industrial equipment, electronic components, knitted goods, textile mill products, radio and TV, tires, work clothes, and automobiles). For the fifteen industries combined there was a small *net increase* in employment from 3,288,200 in 1965 to 3,332,700 in 1971 or 1.4 percent; during the same period, total manufacturing employment in the United States increased by 2.6 percent.[6]

The charge that jobs are being exported usually is related to the activities of multinational corporations. The available data provide little or no support for the allegation that MNCs have been importing finished products from their subsidiaries and thus exporting jobs on balance.[7] There are localized situations where some industries have reduced the number of jobs as imports have increased. However, MNCs generally have experienced a large increase in employment. One analysis concluded that from 1960 to 1970, employment in the United States rose by 12.3 percent and employment in MNCs advanced by almost 37 percent.[8] A Harvard study concluded that "perhaps 600,000 jobs would be lost if there were no foreign investment by MNCs." [9]

Thus, in terms of *actual* employment there is no support for the thesis that there has been a large export of jobs. In this connection, a U.S. Department of Commerce staff study in 1972 concluded: "On the whole then, U.S. foreign direct investment has not been a significant source of job-displacing imports into the United States." [10]

Trade is a two-way affair. If the shifts of production overseas in some industries "export jobs," the goods the affiliates buy in this country must "import jobs." Additional jobs also are created in this country to handle and finance the two-way flow of trade. The suggestion that American companies are producing overseas goods formerly produced here and then have imported those products for sale in this country has limited significance in most areas of the economy.

It is a basic fallacy to assume that production overseas by affiliates is a direct substitute for exports from the United States and that by holding down or eliminating such foreign production, American exports would be increased by the parent company. It ignores the reality that some foreign markets either are closed to imports from the United States or that such imports are subject to severe limitation as foreign governments seek to promote domestic industries.[11] It ignores the fact that lower costs overseas for some products give foreign producers a competitive advantage over U.S. producers and that this can be met only by producing overseas.[12]

The fact that other exports may be stimulated by a foreign subsidiary which opens up new markets for American products also is ignored.[13] Plants established abroad usually produce a limited number of items. Yet the physical presence of the plant in a country combined with a company's local sales and service efforts, storage facilities, and on the spot publicity facilitate the sale of other products by the company. The net result has been an increase in American exports.[14] Thus, overseas investment creates American jobs which provide an offset to any that may be lost if exports are reduced, voluntarily or involuntarily.

THE SHIFTING MERCHANDISE TRADE BALANCE

A major shift in the merchandise balance also has contributed significantly to a revival of protectionism in this country. In the 1960 to 1965 period, annual merchandise exports averaged more than $5 billion above imports.[15] However, by 1968 the export surplus had declined to $635 million, or to the lowest level since the end of World War II. After an increase in the export surplus in 1970, a dramatic change occurred in 1971 when there was *an import surplus* of $2.7 billion; in 1972 imports exceeded exports by $6.9 billion. In 1973, we again had an export surplus.

This shift in the trade balance was *not* due to a decline in exports. Actually, both imports and exports have increased in each year since 1967 (see Table 3-2). However, imports rose more rapidly than exports.

Table 3-2

MERCHANDISE TRADE, 1967–1973
(in billions of dollars)

	Exports	Imports	Net Balance
1967	30.7	26.9	+3.8
1968	33.6	33.0	+.6
1969	36.4	35.8	+.6
1970	42.0	39.8	+2.2
1971	42.8	45.5	−2.7
1972	48.8	55.7	−6.9
1973	70.3	69.5	−.8

Source: *Economic Indicators,* January 1974, p. 24.

THE COMMON MARKET

Common Market trade has been growing rapidly. However, a key element in the Common Market structure is a free movement of goods within the Market and a tariff wall protecting the Market against the outside world. As a result, exports to Common Market countries from member countries rose from 31.9 percent in 1957 to 42.4 percent in 1963 and 48.9 percent in 1970, while imports from member countries increased from 28.3 percent in 1957 to 38.9 percent in 1963 and 48.4 percent in 1970.[16]

With the addition of Britain, Denmark, and Ireland, the area of free trade within the Common Market has been significantly expanded. A recent study estimated that intratrade in the expanded Common Market would increase by $9.2 billion; imports from outsiders would be $3.7 billion lower, and sales of local firms would be $5.5 billion lower than they would have been without this development.[17]

In 1972 the U.S. trade deficit with the Common Market was $0.6 billion in contrast to an average annual surplus of $2.5 billion in the 1960 to 1965 period.[18]

JAPANESE TRADE

The explosive increases in exports to this country from Japan, while access to the Japanese market has been restricted, also has encouraged protectionist sentiment. Imports of electronic products, textiles, steel, and automobiles have risen dramatically and have caused considerable concern in those industries. This concern was translated into agreements to establish "voluntary quotas" on exports of steel and textiles to this country.[19]

Imports from Japan increased from $1.0 billion in 1961 to $5.9 billion in 1970 to $9.1 billion in 1972 while exports to that country increased from $1.8 billion to $4.6 billion to $5.0 billion. As a result, our net balance of trade shifted from a *net export surplus* of $0.8 billion in 1961 to a *net import surplus* of $1.3 billion in 1970 and $4.1 billion in 1972.[20]

There has been some reduction in our *net* import surplus in 1973 as Japan has opened its doors to more American products and has sought to limit its total exports to this country.[21] Early in 1972 Japan agreed to undertake some liberalizations of trade including abolishing their tariff on soybeans, reducing the internal excise tax on large and medium sized automobiles, and removing import quota restrictions on light aircraft and parts and various computer equipment.[22] Despite these recent changes, Japanese trade developments have contributed significantly to the rise in protectionist sentiment.

Causes of Deterioration in U.S. Trade Balance

The shift to a net import surplus in 1971 and 1972 has been attributed to a number of factors, some of which have been overemphasized. The main factors appear to have been (1) the overvalued dollar, (2) the demand for imports in an expanding American economy, and (3) vigorous competition from foreign sellers. On the other hand, two other factors, frequently cited, do not appear to have been too significant: (4) price inflation in the United States appears to have played a minor role in recent years and (5) the trade activities of the MNCs have actually prevented the negative balance from being even larger rather than contributing to it.

OVERVALUED DOLLAR

Prior to the Smithsonian agreement in December 1971, the dollar was overvalued in the world markets with inevitable adverse consequences on the flow of trade. American goods became relatively more expensive to foreign buyers, and as a result, the increase in U.S. exports lagged badly behind free world exports. For example, between 1967 and 1971, U.S. exports increased by 40 percent, while total free world exports increased by 65 percent. Second, imports became relatively less expensive to American buyers because they could buy foreign currencies cheaply.

The depreciation of the dollar since December 1971 already appears to have contributed to a reduction in, and may result in a reversal of, our negative trade balance.[23] However, the initial effect was to increase the trade deficit because of the relatively larger increase in prices for imports. In 1972, import prices increased by 7.5 percent "without an immediate reduction in volume" while export prices rose by only 3.5 percent.[24]

The U.S. Department of Commerce reported in August 1973 that since December 1971 "prices charged by United States manufacturers for their exports have risen only about 7 percent while the prices Americans are paying for imports have risen roughly 24 percent." [25]

A Federal Reserve Board study estimated "that higher prices resulting from changes in exchange rates added between $1 billion and $2 billion to the value of imports in 1972." This increase was offset in part by an estimated decrease of $500 million in demand for imports.[26] In 1973, however, some of the longer-run effects of that depreciation of the dollar were beginning to be evident as the gap between imports and exports first was narrowed significantly and then was changed to an export surplus. The depreciation of the dollar in the first half of 1973 resulted in a rise in import prices and thus acted to increase the total value of imports. In the latter part of the year, the increase in the value of the dollar reversed the earlier decline.

THE EXPANDING AMERICAN ECONOMY

The American economy is the largest in the world, and we have the highest level of living. As a result, it is a magnet for many products. As consumer incomes have expanded, optional spending has increased for a wide variety of foreign products. Small foreign cars early were found to be attractive, and the same has been true for many other consumer products from abroad including shoes, cameras, television sets, and transistor radios. Demand for imports is not limited to consumer products. As our economy has grown, we have required increasing amounts of raw materials from all over the world. Iron ore, bauxite, copper, and petroleum among other products have flowed to this country in increasing volume to meet the needs of our expanding industries. Imports of finished products, such as capital equipment and steel, also have increased in volume.

As demand expands and domestic supplies of key materials cannot keep pace, we must rely increasingly on imports. The latest and what could be one of the most significant illustrations, because of the huge number of dollars involved, is petroleum and its products. Oil quotas limited imports until 1973, but our urgent domestic needs resulted in a removal of this dike to imports. However, the Arab boycott on sales of oil to the United States late in 1973 and the marked increase in prices indicated the danger of excessive reliance on overseas supplies of oil. It resulted in new emphasis upon our becoming more self-sufficient through the combination of conservation measures and the development of alternative sources of energy.

Periods of economic expansion provide an additional stimulus to imports. The combination of higher prices for imports and expanding economic activity resulted in an increase of more than $10 billion in imports in 1972. Two special temporary factors contributed to this record; the catch-up after the 1971 dock strike and the removal of the surtax on imports.[27]

VIGOROUS COMPETITION FROM FOREIGN SELLERS

An important factor contributing to the dramatic rise in imports has been the vigorous and effective competition from foreign sellers. Although it is claimed that MNCs have been importing large quantities of products from their overseas subsidiaries, this source has provided only a minor share of the total.

Actually, the dramatic rise in imports has been from foreign competitors as the increasing numbers of Volkswagens, Toyotas, Sony TV sets, etc. clearly show. The significant rise in steel imports has been from foreign companies in Japan and Western Europe. Textiles have flooded this country from foreign companies in Japan, Korea, Taiwan, and Hong Kong.

These imports have proved popular in this country for several reasons: (1) lower price (e.g. steel, textiles), (2) attractive products (e.g. motorcycles, tape recorders, transistor radios, small-screen television sets, small cars), and (3) workmanship (particularly for Japanese and German products).

RECORD OF MULTINATIONAL COMPANIES

Labor leaders contend that American owned foreign plants displace American exports and that they directly compete with domestic output by shipping products back to the United States.[28] However, studies of the relative significance of imports from foreign affiliates show that on an overall basis they play a minor role in the United States, although they may be important in some industries.

In 1970, for example, *manufacturing imports from majority-owned affiliates* were $4,787 million of which $2,937 million was transportation (autos), largely from Canadian plants. Since manufacturing shipments were $634 billion in 1970, these imports were only about three-quarters of 1 percent of the total in the United States.

Total exports by MNCs have been rising more rapidly than their total imports so that their net export balance has been increasing in contrast to our national experience. A study by the U.S. Department of Commerce showed that the *net export balance* for 298 MNCs *increased* from $5,291 million in 1966 to $7,619 million in 1970.[29] During the same period, the total net export balance for the U.S. *declined* from $3,872 million to $2,176 million.

The record is clear. MNCs have made a positive contribution to the balance of trade. Without that contribution, an import surplus would have developed before 1971 and would have been much larger in subsequent years.

PRICE INFLATION, HERE AND ABROAD

It has often been suggested that the shift in our trade balance has taken place because we have "priced ourselves out of the market." Actually, prices and unit labor costs have risen much less in this country than for most of our trading partners in recent years, as is shown in Tables 3-3 and 3-4.

Table 3-3

INCREASES IN CONSUMER PRICE INDEX
(in percentages)

	1960–1965	1971	1972	1965–1972	1960–1972
U.S.	6.5	4.3	3.3	32.8	41.4
Japan	35.3	6.3	4.8	45.3	96.6
Germany	14.5	5.1	5.8	26.9	45.3
Netherlands	18.0	7.5	7.8	48.1	74.7
United Kingdom	18.9	9.5	7.1	46.6	74.3
Canada	8.4	2.8	4.8	30.1	41.1

Source: International Monetary Fund, *International Financial Statistics,* various issues.

Table 3-4

INCREASES IN UNIT LABOR COSTS IN U.S.
DOLLARS, ANNUAL RATES
(in percentages)

	1960–1965	1971	1972	1965–1972	1960–1972
U.S.	−0.7	−0.2	1.0	3.1	1.8
Japan	4.2	15.3	20.9	6.3	4.1
Germany	3.7	14.3	13.5	7.9	4.8
Netherlands	6.7	12.3	14.0	6.2	5.4
United Kingdom	2.1	9.0	10.8	3.8	2.2
Canada	−2.9	5.6	4.9	4.5	1.9
Expanded Common Market	3.6	11.4	12.8	5.6	3.6

Source: Patricia Capdevielle and Arthur Neef, "Productivity and Unit Labor Costs in 12 Industrial Countries," *Monthly Labor Review,* November 1973, pp. 16, 18.

In 1971 and 1972, the increase in consumer prices in the United States was smaller (with one exception) than in each of the other five countries. Over the longer period of time, a similar pattern emerges. From 1960 to 1965, the United States recorded the best performance. From 1965 to 1972, the rise in consumer prices was moderately higher than in Germany and Canada and much smaller than in Japan and England.

Unit labor costs in manufacturing in the United States *in terms of U.S. dollars* have been increasing far less than in the other countries. In part, this record reflects the depreciation of the dollar since December 1971. However, even in terms of national currencies the rise in unit labor costs in the United States was much smaller than abroad in 1971 and 1972, although it was greater in the United States between 1963 and 1969.[30]

Unit value indexes for exports rose more for the United States than for developed areas from 1963 to 1969 with increases of 15 percent and 8 percent respectively. Between 1969 and the third quarter of 1972, largely because of the devaluation of the dollar, the indexes increased 12.1 percent for the United States and by 20.4 percent for other countries.[31] Moreover, indexes of terms of trade which relate unit value indexes of exports and unit value indexes of imports recorded little change between 1963 and 1969 and then become relatively favorable to the United States in 1972. These indexes provide only rough approximations at best since there are many limitations inherent in their construction.[32]

In light of the foregoing data, the role of price inflation alone appears to have been considerably exaggerated as a cause of our trade balance problem.

TRADE BARRIERS DO NOT DEAL WITH CAUSES
OF TRADE DETERIORATION

One conclusion emerges from this review of the causes of our deteriorating trade balance. The cure is found neither in raising tariffs nor in erecting new nontariff barriers. The overvalued dollar appears to have played a primary role and its significance has been reduced or eliminated by the devaluations in 1971 and 1973. That this was a major cause is indicated by the marked improvement in the trade balance in 1973. The erection of new barriers could act to reduce the flow of goods from abroad. However, the cost would be a lower level of living in this country as lower priced, attractive products either were excluded or became available in more limited quantities or at much higher prices and as this vital source of competitive pressure was reduced. Price inflation has been at a slower rate in this country than for our major trading partners and hence does not provide a reason for erecting new trade barriers. Finally, the record indicates that MNCs have been making increasingly greater contributions to our trade balance.

It is against this background that the proposed Burke-Hartke bill and the proposed Trade Reform Act of 1973 should be evaluated.

The Burke-Hartke Bill

The proposals embodied in the Burke-Hartke bill are even more protectionist than the disastrous Smoot-Hawley Tariff Act of 1930. This legislation is directed mainly against MNCs and their alleged adverse impact on employment, the export of technology, and the balance of payments. The main objectives are to reduce imports sharply through mandatory low quotas and other measures, to control the transfer of technology abroad, and to reduce investment overseas by imposing heavy tax burdens on income earned on those investments. The adoption of these proposals would be an unmitigated disaster. Although the control of overseas investments will have a significant adverse impact upon the volume of foreign trade and the balance of payments, here I shall deal only with the effects of import quotas since direct barriers to trade are the main concern of this analysis.[33]

IMPORT QUOTAS

To correct the alleged adverse employment effects of MNCs, it is proposed to limit all imports drastically by establishing quotas country by country based on the 1965 to 1969 proportions of our imports to domestic output.[34]

An analysis prepared by the staff of the Board of Governors of the Federal Reserve System pointed out that with such a quota for imports, "after allowance for price increases since the base period and assuming no exemptions, the rollback in imports would have been roughly $12 billion. This would be a reduction of about 26 percent from the actual 1971 level of $45.6 billion." [35]

Dr. Arthur Burns, chairman of the Board of Governors, has concluded that "the imposition of quotas conceived in this bill would be an enormous setback for U.S. and world trade." [36]

The Council of Economic Advisers has contrasted the effects of an import quota and a tariff as follows:

The main drawback of a quota as compared to a tariff is that unless a tariff is prohibitive it does not inhibit competition as much as a quota, unless the quota is ineffective. This is so because a tariff allows imported goods to enter if, even with a tariff, they are competitively priced. A tariff therefore puts a limit on the amount by which the domestic price can exceed the world price. An effective quota, on the other hand, does not put any limit on the rise in domestic prices. Those who are permitted to import under a quota system are under no obligation to pass on the lower world price to their customers; their right to import gives them a windfall profit. Under a tariff the difference between the world price and the domestic price accrues to the Treasury.[37]

Economists are virtually unanimous in their rejection of import quotas for a number of good reasons. Import quotas are economically unsound because they result in a lower level of employment and output,[38] restrict growth of companies,[39] encourage retaliation by other nations, restrict consumer choice, increase inflation pressures by reducing supplies, lead to an inefficient allocation of resources, and create additional adverse pressures on the balance of payments.

Moreover, in a dynamic economy, import quotas based on past experience result in inefficiency because they freeze existing patterns of trade. New firms may be given little or no quotas thus removing an important competitive force.

Import quotas now in effect have been very costly to the American consumer. Andrew F. Brimmer, a member of the Federal Reserve Board, reported in 1972:

> Import quotas for *petroleum* now cost the American consumer $5 billion more for oil products.
> *Sugar* quotas cost "in the neighborhood of $300 to $500 million."
> *Textile* quotas cause consumers "to pay about $300 million more than they would have spent on imported items." [40]

He also estimated that *if* automobile quotas had been imposed based on 1966 volume plus 5 percent per year, "consumers might have had to pay $700–$800 million more for automobiles in 1971 than they actually did."

Dr. C. Fred Bergsten of Brookings Institution has estimated that the cost of voluntary quotas was "about $350 million annually" for meat and had raised steel "import prices by an estimated 10 percent." He estimated the total cost of tariff and nontariff restrictions "clearly reaches $10 billion annually and may exceed $15 billion." [41]

The effort to limit imports ignores the fact that if the imported product is lower in price than those produced domestically, consumers can use the savings to buy other products and that such purchases create jobs. Foreign trade permits each country to specialize with attending benefits to consumers in each country. Unfortunately, all of the benefits derived are not easily identifiable because the jobs created are dispersed throughout the economy, while the jobs lost tend to be concentrated in one industry or in a few areas and hence are easily identified. Nevertheless, the gains from international specialization are real and they should be recognized.

Moreover, many foreign products that have captured a part of our market have done so in response to consumer demand. Good illustrations include the transistor radio and small foreign cars. American manufacturers often ignored the demand for such products and foreign producers stepped into the vacuum. Import quotas provide no answer for these situations.

The case against the use of import quotas is overwhelming. Particularly during a period of price inflation, there is no excuse for the adoption of a policy which would add to the burdens of consumers. It is instructive in this connection to note that the Nixon Administration in 1973 announced it would end import restrictions on meat, milk products, and oil as key measures in its efforts to hold down prices. Senator Hartke's World Market Share Act of 1973 would be better named "The Price Raising Act of 1973."

Alternatively it could be called "The Increasing Unemployment Act of 1973" because the proposed restriction on imports and the accompanying decline in exports will result in the loss of many jobs.

Proposed Trade Reform Act of 1973

The proposed Nixon Trade Reform Act of 1973 would make available to the president an arsenal of weapons to deal with foreign trade. The authority proposed may be grouped into three categories:

A. *Free Trade Provisions*
   1. To negotiate reductions in nontariff barriers—Congress must be given prior notification and has the right of veto.
   2. To provide special benefits to workers hurt by imports until a broader program is developed to cover all unemployed.
   3. To extend most favored nation treatment to Communist countries.
   4. To reduce import barriers temporarily to fight price inflation.
   5. To provide no tariff on some products imported from less developed countries.

B. *Protectionist Provisions*
   1. To impose import restrictions and to adopt less restrictive criteria to determine whether to adopt import restraints.
   2. To expedite investigations and decisions re: antidumping duties.
   3. To raise trade barriers including temporary import surcharges, against countries which unreasonably or unjustifiably restrict imports from the United States.

C. *Protectionist or Free Trade*
   1. To eliminate, reduce, or increase tariffs through negotiated agreements.
   2. To raise or lower import restrictions temporarily to aid the balance of payments.

It is evident that this is a mixed bag of policies to increase protection and to make possible greater areas of free trade. Nevertheless, this proposed bill could provide more protection than any act since the Smoot-Hawley Tariff Act of 1930.

ADJUSTMENT ASSISTANCE

Although a liberalization of foreign trade would increase the *total* number of jobs on balance, some workers may be hurt in the process. Assistance to workers who lose jobs when tariffs are lowered must be placed in proper perspective. Workers also may be hurt when production centers shift within the country (e.g. the shift of cotton textile manufacture from New England to the South) or when new technological changes take place (e.g. the airplane and its impact on long distance passenger travel by train) or when natural resources can no longer be efficiently mined (e.g. coal in West Virginia) or when new areas of activity develop in other sections of the country (e.g. the sharp decline in relative importance of the Port of New York) or when new ways of doing business are developed (e.g. the discount house and the supermarket) or when new products are developed (synthetic fibers). In all of these situations and in many others, some workers have lost jobs, but an even larger number of jobs has been created elsewhere in the economy. Such shifts are inevitable so long as we desire to have a dynamic economy.

Moreover, workers also may become unemployed when the government attempts to hold down economic activity in the battle against inflation or as a result of raw-material shortages created by the actions of other countries (e.g. the oil boycott by Arab countries in 1973). I find no reason to give special treatment to those who become unemployed because of foreign trade policy as compared with the much larger number who lose jobs because of government policies affecting other sectors of the economy.

President Nixon appropriately has concluded: "Our responsibilities for easing the problems of displaced persons are not limited to those whose unemployment can be traced to imports." [42] The argument for special treatment only for those workers affected by imports is weak on economic grounds although it has strong rhetorical and political appeal. I believe that the Nixon approach is the proper one, with workers adversely affected by trade negotiations receiving special benefits temporarily at the rates proposed for all unemployed under the longer-range program.

GOALS OF POLICY

Although the Nixon bill is less protectionist than the Burke-Hartke bill, it could represent a significant reversal of the trend toward free trade since 1934. Its adoption would make possible a shift to highly protectionist measures unless the bill's provisions are intended only as a bargaining tool to assist in negotiating lower nontariff barriers in exchange for not implementing the proposed measures. However, the availability of such authority could prove irresistible to an administration which gives heavy weight to political rather than to economic considerations.

The main thrust of foreign trade policy should be to reduce barriers to trade, not to increase them. Every effort must be directed to reduce and to eliminate nontariff barriers which provide the major impediments to trade currently. But international negotiations will not get very far in this direction if Congress authorizes the president to adopt new barriers at the same time. Foreign countries resented our unilateral adoption of temporary surtaxes in 1971 and the imposition of export controls over some farm products in 1973. Against this background other nations understandably could question whether there is any real purpose in entering into serious trade negotiations.

The president should be given the authority he requests to negotiate reductions in tariffs and in nontariff barriers. However, his power to impose restrictive measures should be carefully limited to ensure that they do not become the open door to a major wave of protectionism. Liberal trade policy rather than protectionism is the road to greater economic efficiency and to the more abundant life, as the experience of the past four decades has amply shown.

NOTES

1. Campbell R. McConnell, *Economics,* fifth ed. (New York: McGraw Hill, 1972), p. 770. See also U.S. Tariff Commission estimates reproduced in *United States Commercial Policy: A Program for 1960s* (Washington: Subcommittee on Foreign Economic Policy of the Joint Economic Committee, 87th Congress, 1st Session, 1961), pp. 4, 7.
2. *Economic Report of the President* (Washington, February 1971), p. 154.

3. Gottfried Haberler, "Integration and Growth of the World Economy in Historical Perspective," *The American Economic Review,* March 1964, pp. 13–14.

4. *The New York Times,* September 14, 1973, p. 53.

5. *COPE,* July 3, 1972. For an evaluation, see "Policy Aspects of Foreign Investment by U.S. Multinational Corporations," staff study, in *The Multinational Corporation, Studies on U.S. Foreign Investment* (Washington: U.S. Department of Commerce, March 1972), vol. 1, p. 20 and "Implications of Multinational Firms for World Trade and Investment and for U.S. Trade and Labor" (Washington: U.S. Tariff Commission, January 16, 1973), chap. VII.

6. U.S. Department of Labor, Bureau of Labor Statistics, *Employment and Earnings,* various issues.

7. *Survey of Current Business,* October 1970, p. 20.

8. Eugene D. Jaffe, "In Defense of MNCs: Implications of Burke-Hartke," *MSU Business Topics* (Summer 1973), p. 13.

9. Robert B. Stobaugh, Jose de la Torre, Jr., and Robert C. Ronstadt, "U.S. Multinational Enterprises and the U.S. Economy" in *The Multinational Corporation, Studies on U.S. Foreign Investment,* p. 31. See also Robert G. Hawkins, *U.S. Multinational Investment in Manufacturing and Domestic Economic Performance, Occasional Paper No. 1* (Washington: Center for Multinational Studies, February 1972), p. i.

10. "Policy Aspects of Foreign Investment by U.S. Multinational Corporations," in *The Multinational Corporation, Studies on U.S. Foreign Investment,* vol. 1, p. 22.

11. F. Michael Adler, "The High Cost of Foreign Investment Restraints," *Columbia Journal of World Business,* May–June 1968, p. 77; *The Multinational Corporation, Studies on U.S. Foreign Investment,* vol. 1, p. 23.

12. *The Outlook for Overseas Production and Trade* (New York: The Conference Board, 1969), p. 5.

13. Marie T. Bradshaw, "U.S. Exports to Foreign Affiliates of U.S. Firms," *Survey of Current Business,* May 1969, p. 35.

14. A Bureau of Labor Statistics study found that employment related to exports increased from 2,774,000 in 1963 to 3,665,000 in 1970 and 3,542,00 in 1971; preliminary data indicate the 1972 total was about equal to that in 1970. Donald P. Eldridge and Norman G. Saunders, "Employment and Exports 1963–72," *Monthly Labor Review,* August 1973, pp. 16–27.

15. During this period, exports of services continued to exceed imports of services. It has been suggested that as our economy has become increasingly service oriented, we have been losing our comparative advantage in goods. For an interesting analysis, see John E. Leimone, "Comparative Advantage and the Changing Composition of U.S. Output, Exports, and Imports," *Monthly Review* (Federal Reserve Bank of Atlanta, September 1973), pp. 134–143.

16. *Basic Statistics of the Community* (Luxembourg: Statistical Office of the European Communities, 1965), pp. 108, 110, 112, 114 and *ibid.*, 1971, pp. 82–89.

17. Mordechai E. Kreinin, "Development in International Trade: 1973," *MSU Business Topics,* Summer 1973, p. 50.

18. *Weekly Report, Congressional Quarterly* (Washington: May 19, 1973), p. 1215.

19. For an excellent discussion of "voluntary" exports agreements with Japan and with other countries see Malcolm D. H. Smith, "Voluntary Export Quotas and U.S. Trade Policy—A New Non-Tariff Barrier," *Law and Policy in International Business,* 5, no. 1 (Washington: Georgetown University Law Center, 1973), pp. 10–55.

20. "United States Foreign Trade 1961–1967" (Annual) (Washington: U.S. Department of Commerce, Bureau of International Commerce, May 1968); *Overseas Business Reports,* May 1968, p. 17; and *Survey of Current Business,* March 1972, p. 41 and March 1973, p. 29.

21. In the first eight months of 1973, the import surplus was $1.15 billion as compared with $2.72 billion a year earlier (*The New York Times,* October 4, 1973).

22. *Hearings on 1972 Economic Report of the President* (Washington: U.S. Joint Economic Committee, 92nd Congress, 2nd Session, 1972), Part 2, pp. 348–349.

23. According to the U.S. Department of Commerce, "the delayed positive impact of the 1971 devaluation may now be offsetting the initial perverse effect on imports of the February 1973 devaluation. . . ." (*Survey of Current Business,* June 1973, p. 23).

24. *Survey of Current Business,* March 1973, p. 29.

25. *The New York Times,* August 5, 1973, Section 3, p. 7.

26. *Federal Reserve Bulletin,* April 1973, pp. 249–250.

27. The U.S. Department of Commerce estimated that "labor disturbances . . . were probably responsible for less than one-fifth of the 1971 deterioration in the trade balance" (*Survey of Current Business,* March 1972, p. 38).

28. George Meany, *A Modern Trade Policy for the Seventies* (Washington: American Federation of Labor and Congress of Industrial Organizations, 1972), pp. 8–9; and Nat Goldfinger, *COPE*, July 3, 1972.

29. *Special Survey of U.S. Multinational Companies, 1970* (Washington: U.S. Department of Commerce, November 1972), p. 87 and Table 5. See also *The Effects of U.S. Corporate Foreign Investment, 1960–1970* (New York: Business International Corp., November 1972), pp. 5, 22; and *Plain Words . . .* (Washington: Emergency Committee for American Trade, 1972).

30. *Economic Report of the President* (Washington: Council of Economic Advisers, January 1972), p. 152.

31. *Economic Report of the President* (Washington: Council of Economic Advisers, January 1973), p. 300.

32. See Irving B. Kravis and Robert E. Lipsey, *Price Competitiveness in World Trade* (New York: Columbia University Press, 1971), pp. 3–7.

33. The argument for higher taxes is found in Arnold Cantor, "Tax Subsidies that Export Jobs," *AFL-CIO American Federationist*, November 1972. For critical evaluations and data, see *Economic Implications of Proposed Changes in the Taxation of U.S. Investments Abroad* (New York: Foreign Trade Council Inc., June 1972), pp. 5–14; *New Proposals for Taxing Foreign Income* (New York: National Association of Manufacturers, August 1971); *Union Carbide's International Investment Benefits the U.S. Economy* (New York: Union Carbide Corp., October 1972).

34. *World Market Share Act of 1973*, Section 201, introduced January 18, 1973.

35. *Hearings on the 1972 Economic Report of the President* (Washington: Joint Economic Committee, 1972), p. 185.

36. *Ibid.*, p. 183.

37. *Economic Report of the President* (Washington: February 1971), p. 156.

38. Alcoa has warned that "if the quota system cuts back the foreign bauxite and alumina vital to Alcoa's U.S. operations, it will directly cut back stateside Alcoa jobs" ("The Burke-Hartke Bill, Can It Save American Jobs," *Alcoa News*, May 1972, p. 5).

39. According to American Cyanamid, "setting arbitrary levels of imports based on past experience would inhibit the company's growth in any area that might require future import of raw materials or intermediates" (American Cyanamid Corp., *The Burke-Hartke Bill*, January 26, 1972, p. 16).

40. Andrew F. Brimmer, *Imports and Economic Welfare in the United States* (New York: Foreign Policy Association, February 16, 1972), pp. 19–23.
41. C. Fred Bergsten, *The Cost of Import Restrictions to American Consumers* (New York: American Importers Association, 1972).
42. *Congressional Quarterly*, April 14, 1973, p. 853.

FOUR

Multinational Enterprises:
Performance and Accountability *

Raymond Vernon

*Herbert F. Johnson Professor of
International Business Management
Graduate School of Business Administration
Harvard University*

It is taking a little time for scholars and statesmen to absorb some
of the implications of the mushrooming growth of multinational
enterprises. Not for lack of trying, it is clear. The flood of words on
the subject, printed and verbal, has been quite overwhelming in the
past few years. But the flood simply reflects a deeply felt need on the
part of national leaders to get a handle on a slippery and amorphous
issue, rather than progress on the issue itself.

The difficulties in coming to grips with the issue are not at all surprising. The structure of the multinational enterprise is revolutionary; it is a structure that sits awkwardly in a global system which is
based on the building blocks of the nation-state. Though a few illus-

* The research on which this paper is based was financed mainly by grants from
the Ford Foundation to the Harvard Business School and to Harvard's Center
for International Affairs.

trations of such enterprises could be found seventy-five or one
hundred years ago, the flowering of this particular form of enterprise
did not occur until after World War II. The implications of these
developments are sufficiently recent and sufficiently profound that a
certain amount of time is needed for reflection and perspective.

TWO FACES OF THE MULTINATIONAL ENTERPRISE

The multinational enterprise can be looked on from many different points of view. Two are particularly revealing. One, an outsider's
view, sees the multinational enterprise as a group of corporations
of various nationalities, joined together by ties of ownership. A parent located in one country and invested with the nationality of that
country acts as the owner of various foreign subsidiaries and branches
endowed with other nationalities. When the constituent units of the
group are managed in accordance with some common strategy, and
when they draw upon some common pool of money, knowledge, skill,
and influence, they are thought of collectively as a multinational
enterprise. EXXON, Pechiney, British Petroleum, Ciba, and several
hundred other organizations fit this pattern.

On first blush, there is nothing very revolutionary about such an
organization. But one has to bear in mind what a modern corporation is. Though different jurisdictions have developed different
treatments for the modern corporation, practically all jurisdictions
have endowed these entities with many of the rights and attributes
of natural persons, such as the right to own and to owe, and the right
to sue and be sued. When these powers reside in a corporation they
have vastly greater potential power than when they reside in a natural person: first, because the corporation is usually immortal,
created without limit of time; second, because it is expansible, that
is, because it normally has both the legal rights and the organizational
structure that will permit it to grow without limit; third, because it
has remarkable capacities for reproduction and fusion, being em-
powered as a rule to absorb other corporations as well as to create
offspring or parents.

These attributes alone would make the modern corporation a formidable institution. But there are still others. Though corporations may be linked together by ties of ownership and management, each unit has a separate identity under law. As a rule, each unit is responsible only for its own acts and liabilities, not for the acts and liabilities of any other unit in the enterprise. Moreover, each unit derives its nationality from the sovereign that created it. While sharing common resources and responding to a common strategy, the constituent units nevertheless can claim the rights and exploit the advantages of corporate separateness, including the rights that go with nationality.

It is true, of course, that the rights of corporations which are under the control of foreigners are sometimes circumscribed by the state in special ways. Foreign-owned corporations, for instance, are often excluded from especially sensitive business activities, such as radio broadcasting, ordnance production, and coastal shipping; they are often denied access to governmental subsidies, especially those intended to stimulate research and innovation; and they are commonly subjected to special regulatory pressures, such as limitations on their rights to use foreign personnel or foreign materials in the course of their business activities.[1] Still, such corporations are generally entitled to most of the rights and privileges that are available to artificial entities in the jurisdiction that created them. For instance, a Japanese corporation that is controlled by a U.S. parent may have special difficulty in selling its products to the Japanese government and may have no chance at all of getting state subsidies to support its research efforts; but its run-of-the-mill rights as a Japanese national will still be respected and enforced.

In sharp contrast to this external view of the multinational enterprise is a second view, the perception of those working inside the organization. When multinational enterprises organize themselves to do business, they try to choose the form of structure and the kind of relationships among their various corporate units and branches that seem most conducive to the business purpose of the enterprise as a whole. If there is a pool of common resources to be shared and a nub of common strategy to be pursued, the operating organization must be shaped in such a way as to reflect these facts. Sometimes the corporate units that are the formal building blocks of the multinational enterprise retain their separate identities in the operating organization; but more often, the boundaries that formally distinguish the corporate units prove quite irrelevant in the course of actual operations.

Consider the characteristic organizational evolution of multinational enterprises, at least of those with U.S. parents.[2] As a matter of history, such enterprises were usually organized at first to respond to the needs of their U.S. market. In the majority of cases, this has meant that once the enterprise attained a certain size, the primary division inside the organization serving the U.S. market was based on distinctions by products: the management of fertilizers was separated from that of plastics, plastics from dyestuffs, dyestuffs from drugs, and so on.

After the Second World War, as business grew in foreign markets and as overseas subsidiaries were created, the first instinct of large U.S. organizations was to assign such offshore business to a single distinctive unit in the organization, an international division that sat outside of the main organizational structure. That unit was usually placed under the guidance of an international vice president, who in turn tapped the resources of the U.S. divisions as needed.

Up to that point in the development of the multinational enterprise, the strategies pursued in different foreign markets could easily maintain major elements of national distinctiveness, especially if the international vice president found it useful to subdivide his own task by countries. Accordingly, the products, the technologies, the channels of distribution, and the personnel policies of a given subsidiary in, say, France or Italy or Britain could remain distinctively French or Italian or British if the vice president thought it desirable. In the next phase of organizational development, however, both the feasibility and the desirability of maintaining such national distinctions tended to decline.

As the experience of multinational enterprises grew, the key executives of such enterprises found themselves thinking in terms of strategies that transcended individual states. One result was that the job of the international vice president characteristically was abolished and his task apportioned out to the rest of the organization. In most cases, the product divisions that had formerly concentrated their world mainly on the U.S. market were given global responsibility; in others, the global market was divided up into large regional areas, each area being typically made up of a considerable number of countries. In both situations, individual countries were submerged in larger units.

Even at this stage, of course, distinctions between countries were not altogether overlooked. Individual countries, after all, still had their own tax laws, labor legislation, tariff structures, and so on. But as a rule, such national distinctions became second-order factors in the strategies and structures of multinational enterprises. What mattered most was product or region. As a result, the key men in the line organization of multinational enterprises came more and more to think of themselves as plastics or drug or dye men, or as Latin American or European or Asian executives.

The evolution that I have just sketched is somewhat better documented for multinational enterprises with U.S. parents than for those with parents in Europe or Japan. But the evidence is beginning to build up that similar tendencies are developing for the European firms.[3] And it is only a matter of time before a like development is discerned in the Japanese moves toward multinationalization.[4]

How much, one may ask, did the preoccupation with a product or the commitment to a large region attenuate the national identification of the business managers involved? To what extent do nationals in the home office continue to identify with their home government, and to what extent do local managers abroad identify with the nation from which they derive their nationality? This is a question remarkably devoid of hard evidence, and packed with unsupported generalizations. All that one can say is that men in all vocations are commonly required to manage and reconcile the conflicts among many different loyalties. A single individual can simultaneously be committed to the Republican party, the United Nations Association, the Ford Motor Company, the Sierra Club, the Planned Parenthood Association, and the Catholic church. The notion that U.S. nationals identify with U.S. interests, Brazilian nationals with Brazilian interests, and so on, is unrealistic on several counts: first, in its assumption that personal identification is so simply made; second, in its assumption that the interests of any given nation are so unambiguously recognized and acknowledged.

My assumption is that, when the subject has been adequately researched, it will suggest some exceedingly complex processes of identification. An American, it may be, will characteristically respond somewhat differently from an Englishman or an Italian. But the power of that well-known refrain, "Let's do it the company way" will represent a strong cohesive force that blurs the distinctiveness of national behavior.[5]

The point can be pushed too far, of course. U.S. executives run- ing U.S.-based enterprises may well appeal to the U.S. government if they see some advantage to be gained in such an appeal, but my assumption is that they will appeal almost as readily to the Swedish or Yugoslav or Brazilian government if they think such an appeal would be equally useful. U.S. executives may not be wholly insensi- tive to pressures emanating from the U.S. government, but my as- sumption is that they would respond almost as readily to the pres- sures of the Mexican or Spanish government, if the pressures were as severe.

As for the behavior of European and Japanese executives who di- rect multinational enterprises from their respective home territories, my starting conjectures are very much the same. All are prepared to be eclectic in their relationships and identifications with various governments, as the needs of their enterprises require. Those execu- tives who direct multinational enterprises headquartered in small open societies such as Switzerland, Sweden, and the Netherlands are better conditioned to such a line of conduct than those from large countries or from societies with a strong ethnocentric propensity; the French or the Japanese, for instance, might well feel a stronger pull to their respective home governments than the Germans or the Italians.

I cannot pretend that these are solid propositions, adequately tested against hard evidence. The material that supports conclusions of this sort is mainly anecdotal and casual.[6] Tested or not, this kind of working hypothesis is bound to spark a note of moral indignation in some. There are those who will see it as an affirmation of their worst suspicions about business executives, and there are others who will see it as an unwarranted attack on business executives. It is, of course, neither. I would apply the very same working hypothesis to the key executive of other transnational institutions: to the key men in United Nations organizations, to the leaders of international labor unions, to the managers of international commodity agree- ments, and so on. A major exception to the generalization would be the men placed in international organizations by totalitarian national governments; these are men operating on a short leash and a choke collar, men whose loyalty must be unambiguous in order to survive. For nationals of other countries, however, the problem of conflicting loyalties is likely to generate seemingly ambiguous responses.

THE PERFORMANCE OF MULTINATIONAL ENTERPRISES

Multinational enterprises come in a wide range of shapes and sizes. But there are certain characteristics that tend to set them apart from enterprises in general. Multinational enterprises are rare in such industries as textiles, furniture, and printing. Such enterprises appear as a rule in industries that are oligopolistic in character, that is, industries in which formidable barriers exist in the entry of newcomers and in which the competing firms are few in number. Accordingly, multinational enterprises tend to be very large firms. Indeed the very largest U.S. firms almost always qualify as multinational enterprises, according to the usual definitions.[7]

Beyond those statements, however, simple generalizations do not come easily. The effects of multinational enterprises differ considerably, according to various characteristics of the enterprise and of the environment in which it operates. Enterprises that derive their oligopoly strength from some special technological strength have rather different effects, as a rule, from those that depend on sheer bigness as an economic advantage; and those that rely on large-scale production facilities have different effects from those that operate on the advantages afforded by trade names or advertising alone. Moreover, there are differences in effects which are associated with time: after a foreign subsidiary has been performing some well-defined task of production or distribution for an extended period, the advantages accruing to the local economy from the continuation of that unchanging task are likely to decline.

Despite the variations, there are still some generalizations worth making. One is that, where some valid basis for comparison exists between multinational enterprises and national enterprises in terms of sheer economic efficiency, the multinational enterprises seem to come out a bit ahead.[8] At times, both types of enterprises adopt policies that seem less than ideal in efficiency terms. In industries that depend on product differentiation, such as automobiles or radios, there are often too many enterprises in the market to permit a proper exploitation of scale economies.[9] In poor countries, large enterprises of all sorts, foreign or local, seem to avoid labor-using techniques rather more than the visible economic facts would suggest desirable.[10] But when all the bits and pieces of evidence are added up, they lend support to the generalization that the multinational enterprise generally performs efficiently as compared with the available alternatives.

Who benefits from this efficiency? The debate on the subject has been much more extensive than the hard research. The debate has been conducted at many different levels. For some disputants, the question itself is irrelevant. Economic efficiency is not what the world is all about; what matters is independence or participation or freedom or revolution. Multinational enterprises need to be judged according to their effects on goals such as these. Others find the question of efficiency germane, but want to know how that efficiency is manifested, whether in more soft drinks or more medicines, in schools or in guns. Many suspect that multinational enterprises determine the output mix and that the mix they create is less than optimal from a social point of view.[11]

Unfortunately, the evidence on these subjects is practically nonexistent. Although Galbraith may be right that big enterprises are in a position to determine the world's demands, no one can say what the structure of those demands would be under alternative systems; Libya's preference for Mirages and the Soviet Union's acceptance of Pepsi-Cola are not strongly supportive of the proposition that socialist economies are in a position to generate a more useful basket of goods and services. In any case, the relative values that observers place on different bundles of outputs are highly subjective. Where rival values are at war, the role of scholarship in the dispute is greatly circumscribed.

Despite all the caveats, the research materials on the multinational enterprise are very rich, and getting richer every day. They encourage the scholar to hope that he can make a contribution, perhaps a critical contribution, to an understanding of the multinational enterprise. Already they indicate firmly that neither the inspired caricatures of the multinational enterprise that are generated by the New Left, nor the saccharine portraits that are produced by the public relations departments of various business organizations have much to do with reality.

Though the scholar can get a reasonably good fix on some of the operations of multinational enterprises, he dare not paint his picture too simply. Consider the critical question: who benefits? A number of major statistical sources happen to shed more than the usual amount of light on the experience of U.S.-based multinational enterprises in the year 1966. And happily for the scholar, various signs point to the conclusion that the performance of that year was not untypical.

In 1966, U.S.-based multinational enterprises reported that some $100 billion of sales had been effected through their five thousand or so affiliates and branches abroad engaged in manufacturing or in the petroleum industry.[12] One cannot say for certain how much of that total represented value added by the affiliate or value added by the local economy as a whole, as distinguished from imported inputs; nevertheless, some elements can be identified, as shown in Table 4-1. For instance, the local employees of these enterprises received $14.7 billion in compensation, while local governments garnered taxes of $10.2 billion, making an identifiable total of $25 billion for the local economy. In addition, there was some considerable use of raw materials and services acquired from local sources, bringing the total value added from local sources to a much higher figure, say, $70 or $75 billion.

What of the direct contributions of these enterprises to the U.S. economy? In 1966, the same group of companies brought back to the United States something like $3.8 billion in dividends, interest and branch earnings, royalties, fees and charges.[13] Judging from the reports of the U.S. Treasury Department, the $3.8 billion returned to the United States generated a trivial amount of taxes for the U.S. government, something less than $1 billion; under the U.S. tax system, the credits granted to these enterprises for payment of foreign

Multinational Corporations

Table 4-1

SELECTED PAYMENTS BY FOREIGN AFFILIATES
OF U.S. ENTERPRISES, 1966
(billions of U.S. dollars)

	Manufac-turing	Petro-leum	Total
To host countries			
Taxes	3.3	6.9	10.2
Payrolls	13.1	1.6	14.7
To U.S.			
Taxes, through parent	0.4	0.3	0.7
Dividends to parent and			
branch earnings	1.3	1.7	3.0
Interest, royalties, other			
fees to parent	0.8	0.1	0.9

Source: Estimates of Harvard Multinational Enterprise Study, based on data of
U.S. Treasury Department and U.S. Commerce Department.

taxes were high enough to offset practically all the increased corporate tax liability that would otherwise be associated with the
returned income.[14] As far as the U.S. government was concerned,
any increase in its revenues had to come mainly from the increased
income received by individuals in the United States as a direct result of the overseas activities of the U.S.-based multinational enterprises. Part of that income went to managers and stockholders, yielding perhaps $2 billion in added tax revenues. Part went to the U.S.
employees of the multinational enterprises, yielding a much less
determinate amount. Add to figures of this sort something like $6
billion of goods purchased from U.S. parents and affiliates. Taken
all together, the direct contribution to the U.S. economy of these
overseas affiliates of U.S. enterprises come to a figure on the order
of $10 billion, as compared with the $70 or $75 billion for foreign
economies mentioned earlier.

Where do calculations of this sort leave us? They are still several
steps removed from the question, Who benefits? The benefit, after

all, is determined not by the gross receipts of the various parties as presented here, but by the net effect upon the parties which arose out of the existence of the multinational enterprise. If the workers in the host country who were employed by the subsidiaries of foreign-owned enterprises would otherwise have been idle, for example, then their total income from the enterprise is a relevant measure of their improved position; but if workers would otherwise have held another job in the host country, then the effect of the multinational enterprise is only the difference between the actual experience of the workers and the alternative employment. The same is true for the gross income of the home government; whether it benefited and how much depends partly on the alternatives created. The taxes collected by the home government directly or indirectly from the overseas subsidiaries' operations may represent no net benefit at all to the home government if such taxes were offset by a loss of revenue that would otherwise have come from activities at home. The same is true for the stockholders receiving dividends and other income.

I see no strong guides, intuitive or empirical, for picturing the alternative state of affairs that would have existed in the absence of the multinational enterprise. There are suggestive indications that some of the activities of the subsidiaries of multinational enterprise in host countries represent additions rather than displacements to the activities of those countries, but generalizations of this sort have to be qualified according to the country, the industry and the stage in the history of the foreign investment.[15] There are also some hints that the activities of multinational enterprises may be additive for the U.S. economy as well; but here, too, the risks of overgeneralization are strong. Nonetheless, data of the sort I have just presented seem to me to shed some light. They reinforce my impression that foreign host countries are the major beneficiaries of the operations of U.S.-based multinational enterprises. Stockholders in the home country obviously profit as well, but government and labor in the home country have to rely on more indirect channels for their benefits.

The question of the distribution of benefits is of intrinsic importance in its own right. But the issue is even more important as an illustration of the danger of applying simple caricatures to the multinational enterprise. It is not the chosen instrument in an international conspiracy for grinding the faces of the poor; neither is it mankind's salvation in a parlous world of hostile nation-states. It is one more human institution, at the same time fallible and useful, whose benefits can be increased and drawbacks reduced by appropriate public policies.

THE QUESTION OF ACCOUNTABILITY

Responsibility and Accountability

Most managers of multinational enterprises approach the issue of social responsibility with a touch of genuine indignation. They see themselves as engaged in an unending process of adapting to the requirements of various jurisdictions, modifying their practices and curbing their preferences in order to conform to the demands of sovereign states. From time to time, they may avoid the impact of some sovereign command by moving beyond the sovereign's reach. From time to time, too, they may find themselves navigating between the conflicting and irreconcilable commands of different states. But most managers will assert with seemingly genuine conviction that illegal evasion is comparatively rare, especially when measured against the practices of indigenously owned competitors; and insofar as there is evidence in this obscure and murky field, there is no reason to reject that generalization.

Nevertheless, a great deal has been written in recent years about the responsibility of managers to measure up to social standards beyond those imposed by sovereign command.[16] Much of what has been written on the subject is special pleading; but some of it is fairly objective stuff. Despite the earnestness and dedication of many of the discussants, I see very little progress in the formulation of an operational concept of social responsibility. As in every other calling, including politics, academia, horseracing, and the arts, business has produced its quota of decent men and its quota of rascals. The very discussion of social responsibility may well have sharpened the sensibilities of some of those who in any case were disposed to identify themselves with social needs; but I doubt that it has done much more. The hard questions still remain unanswered: Should businessmen who produce a much criticized product, such as cigarettes, liquidate a business that is both legal and profitable? Should businessmen whose facilities pollute the atmosphere take on the extra costs of prevention, even though the step may threaten their competitive position in the market?

The problem of the multinational enterprise in defining its social responsibilities is compounded even further. It is not inevitable that the social objectives of one country will be in conflict with the social objectives of another. But conflict is not always avoidable in such matters as full employment, access to raw materials, balance-of-payment stability, national defense, and many other issues. In such cases, whose social objectives are to be served?

Apart from conflicts in the social objectives of nations, there may also be conflicts between what is good for mankind as a whole and what is good for each country taken one at a time. For mankind as a whole, a slow rate of economic growth may conceivably be desirable, but few individual states would identify their interests in this way. Assuming that a multinational enterprise was eager to be responsive to mankind's global interests, it is not clear where it could turn for a definition of those interests, and less clear still how it could handle any conflicts with the social interests of the individual states as these states define such interests.

I have no great expectations of improving the social performance of multinational enterprises by defining and inculcating concepts of social responsibility. But I see real possibilities in a narrower and more explicit approach, namely, increasing the social accountability of such enterprises.[17] The difference between social responsibility and social accountability, as the terms are used here, is profound. The social accountability of the multinational enterprise would be achieved if appropriate social institutions were in a position to make judgments regarding the adequacy of the performance of the enterprises, and were in a position to take remedial measures when they saw some lack. To advance the idea of social accountability, however, one has to develop a set of institutions that for the most part do not exist today.

Policies of Social Accountability

The institutions charged with ensuring that multinational enterprises were appropriately accountable would find themselves, almost at once, wrestling with some of the problems that already have been raised. Would their mandate be that of identifying and reconciling the conflicts in social goals among member states, or would they strive to define social goals in terms of global welfare? In most fields, I suspect, the goal of reconciling national goals would be difficult enough, while the object of contributing to global welfare would be quite out of reach.

It also seems implausible to expect that any single intergovernmental institution could effectively cover all the problems either of reconciling national conflicts or of formulating global goals. The range of problems involved is as broad as the field in industrial policy, a notoriously wider-ranging subject. It includes such issues as tax policies for business, subsidization policies for industrial innovation or industrial adaptation or regional development, policies toward competition and monopoly, and policies in labor relations. Beyond these well-trod areas of industrial policy, moreover, there are also questions that apply especially to the multinational enterprise. These include defining the rights and obligations of multinational enterprise in invoking the powers or responding to the commands of sovereign states, when the interests of some other state are vitally involved. That issue is involved whenever a company approaches its government for help in a foreign country, and whenever a government directs one of its national enterprises to act or to refrain from acting in some manner outside its home territory.

To illustrate the scope and variety of the approaches that may be needed, one has only to consider what some of the objectives in each of these fields ought to be.

In the field of taxation, several objectives would presumably be high on an international agenda, each of them requiring highly technical and detailed agreements.[18] One would be to ensure that multinational enterprises did not slip between the taxing jurisdictions, that is, to ensure that their aggregate income was adequately taxed in some jurisdiction. This could require international agreements that restrained the creation of tax safe havens, or agreements that had the effect of limiting their attractiveness.[19] It could also involve the international pooling or exchange of tax information on the financial activities of the affiliates of multinational enterprise, a step that could increase the efficiency of all the taxing jurisdictions involved. A second objective would be to avoid gross inequities in the distribution of taxable income among the various affiliates of any multinational enterprise, that is, to ensure that a profit which ought to be attributed to one subsidiary is not assigned in effect to another. And a third objective would be to protect the multinational enterprise itself from being caught between the scissors of the taxing jurisdictions, that is, to ensure that the tax laws and regulations of the different jurisdictions were sufficiently compatible so as to avoid the risk of confiscatory taxation. As national taxing jurisdictions grow more sophisticated and more efficient with regard to multinational enterprises, this problem is bound to grow. Each of these objectives would require the development of fairly technical agreements, to be developed and overseen by a specialized international apparatus.

The issue of national subsidies also promises to grow more acute. The questions here are already quite familiar, partly as a result of the experiences of the European Economic Community. In effect, different national jurisdictions are in competition for enterprises that generate jobs. Tax exemptions, subsidies, or outright capital grants are offered in the competition. The sought-after enterprises generally benefit from the competition; labor may also benefit in the country that wins out; but in the country from which the investment is diverted, both labor and government are liable to loss. Outside the European Economic Community, there has been an occasional salvo by some aggrieved country, such as the action of the U.S. government in threatening dumping duties on tires produced by a Michelin plant in Nova Scotia for shipment to the United States. More actions of this sort are probably in the making. This is, of course, a classic area for international regulation, though one quite different in technical content and administrative needs from the field of taxation.

The problems of international competition and monopoly power offer still another field for action.[20] The emergence of the multinational enterprise has had some fundamental implications in this field. In some respects, as enterprises have thrust their way into foreign markets, competition has been fostered; on the other hand, as enterprises have linked up in international alliances and partnerships, the opposite effect has also occurred. In any case, it is no longer realistic to address the problems of oligopolistic practices on a country-by-country basis: in oil, chemicals, electronics, automobiles, copper, aluminum, and other major industries, the oligopolistic structure is global. Whatever the competition policies of individual governments may be, a realistic course of action must take into account the other main markets of the world. Once again, some fairly specialized agreements and specialized apparatus are called for, covering such problems as the sorting out of jurisdictions, the collection of information, and the institution of effective remedies.[21]

The labor relations field may demand a quite different approach. In this case, the growth of multinational enterprises has stimulated its own countervailing force, manifested by the strengthening of various international labor unions.[22] In a few well-publicized cases, the unions in a number of countries have coordinated their negotiations with a common multinational employer; this has occurred so far in cases involving electronics, glass, automobiles, and chemicals. The limitations on this approach, however, may prove fairly formidable. In some situations, to be sure, labor organizations in different countries have an incentive to cooperate in their bargaining, notably when they hope that cooperative conduct will improve the position of all of them. But the different national labor organizations also have interests that are antithetical at times. In some cases, the conflict derives from a difference in their perception of what a labor organization is for. The Communist labor unions of Europe, for instance, may be much more interested in fostering socialism than in improving working conditions at the plant level. In other cases, the conflict may be more explicit and immediate, as when two countries are competing for the added jobs that a multinational enterprise is planning to create. As a result, it is harder to think of cooperation between, say, Mexican and U.S. labor than between Canadian and U.S. labor. In this field, the objective of social accountability may demand no particular action on the part of governments for the present, except perhaps the encouragement of an increased flow of information across national boundaries regarding those activities of the various affiliates of each multinational enterprise that may have a bearing on labor's interests.

Labor groups are not the only national entities that have a need to know something about the operations of affiliates which lie outside their own national arena. Governmental agencies, public investors, consumer watchdog groups, and other national interests also have such needs from time to time. Needs of this sort are so varied and so extensive that it seems almost quixotic to attempt to satisfy them. Yet the present situation is so far from being responsive to such needs that some first steps of a rather obvious sort seem desirable. As matters now stand, each national jurisdiction collects the data it needs, limiting itself as a rule to the activities of the affiliates in its jurisdiction. Anyone interested in the multinational system as a whole, therefore, is hard put to find a central source that describes it. Even the relatively advanced U.S. disclosure requirements, embodied in the various securities statutes, do a poor job of describing the activities of many affiliates located outside of the country.[23] Here, too, is a field in which international agreements have a role to play. Some sort of international clearing house for information that is compiled from official national sources is a possibility. Once again, however, the organizational requirements for carrying out such an operation would set such an activity aside from those discussed earlier.

One of the most difficult problems to be faced in increasing the social accountability of multinational enterprises is how to place a layer of insulation between parent enterprises and their national governments. The object would be to curb the parents' rights to call on their governments for the support of overseas subsidiaries, and at the same time to reduce the ability of governments to influence the action of foreign subsidiaries by commands to the parent.

The delicacy of this problem is obvious. Governments are quite unlikely to accept self-denying ordinances of this sort unless the reciprocal advantages are crystal clear. Accordingly, I would anticipate that progress could be made on this front only among groups of countries with similar interests and outlooks, and only in certain specified fields. If international agreements could be reached in some of the fields mentioned, such as taxation, competition policy, and corporate disclosure, it might be possible for some of the participants to agree among themselves that in such areas the jurisdiction of each stopped at its national borders.

LATIN AMERICA: A SPECIAL PROBLEM

The United States is confronted with a special challenge in its relations with Latin America, a challenge which it might yet turn into an opportunity. Conditioned by a long history of disputes over foreign investment, the Latin American governments have refused to become signatories to the International Convention on the Settlement of Investment Disputes. Their position, hardened by half a century of controversy with the U.S. government, is that business entities operating in any national jurisdiction, although owned by foreigners, are entitled to the rights and subject to the obligations of any other national in that jurisdiction; hence a U.S.-owned subsidary in Latin America would be performing an act of national treachery if it appealed to the U.S. government, a foreign power, for support against the national government that gave the subsidiary its juridical personality.

The argument has merit. It would have even more merit if one could be sure that the regulatory processes of Latin American governments did not discriminate against these entities by reason of their foreign ownership. The administrative systems of Latin America make much greater use of the pragmatic case-by-case approach and much lesser use of general rules than do the legal systems of North America and northern Europe; hence, Latin American governments could easily discriminate on the basis of ownership, while yet remaining within the framework of their existing law and practice.

The elements of a political bargain are present in this situation, though it is a bargain that would not be easy for either party. The United States might acknowledge the validity of the Latin American position, the so-called Calvo doctrine. The Latin American governments might then feel free to accept the jurisdiction of some international tribunal wherever the dispute turned on the question whether discrimination was being practiced against a national enterprise by reason of its foreign ownership. Agreements along these lines would represent something of an achievement in the complex process of increasing the social accountability of multinational enterprises.

NOTES

1. INTEL, *Estudio de la Legislacion Applicable a las Empresas de Capital Multinacional en Areas de Integracion Economica* (Buenos Aires:

INTEL, Interamerican Development Bank, 1970), pp. 179–327; OECD Industry Committee, "Information on Multinational Companies: United States" (Paris: 1970), IMD (70)3/07 Part II, mimeo.

2. The best single source on this subject is J. M. Stopford and L. T. Wells, Jr., *Managing the Multinational Enterprise* (New York: Basic Books, 1972).

3. Summarized in L. G. Franko, "Organizational Change in European Enterprise: The Move toward the Multi-Divisional Structure" (Geneva: Centre d'Etudes Industrielles, July 1973), unpublished.

4. See, for instance, Yoshi Tsurumi, "Japanese Multinational Firms," *Journal of World Trade Law,* 7, no. 1 (January–February 1973), 74–90.

5. That view is shared in part by at least one former U.S. businessman with broad international experience. See E. P. Lions, "The Anational Corporation," unpublished Ph.D. thesis (Geneva: Institut Universitaire des Hautes Etudes Internationales, 1972).

6. See my "Multinational Enterprise and National Security," *Adelphi Papers* (London: Institute for Strategic Studies, March 1971), pp. 1–4.

7. The relationship is well established in numerous studies and is being explored in even more detail in a doctoral thesis by J. W. Vaupel, Kennedy School of Government, Harvard University.

8. For a relevant bibliography, see J. H. Dunning, "The Determinants of International Production," *Oxford Economic Papers,* vol. 25, November 1973.

9. Jack Baranson, *Automotive Industries in Developing Countries* (Baltimore: John Hopkins Press, 1969), pp. 13–53.

10. A balanced presentation of the point, together with copious bibliography, appears in W. A. Chudson and L. T. Wells, Jr., "The Acquisition of Proprietary Technology by Developing Countries from Multinational Enterprises: A Review of Issues and Policies," United Nations, June 1973, restricted and preliminary.

11. Theotonio dos Santos, *El nuevo caracter de la dependencia* (Santiago, Chile: Centro de Estudios Socio-Economicos, Universidad de Chile, 1963), and *Dependencia economica y alternativas de cambio on America Latina* (Santiago, Chile: Centro de Estudios Socio-Economicos, 1970); also S. H. Hymer, "The Efficiency (Contradictions) of Multinational Corporations," *The American Economic Review,* 60, no. 2 (May 1970), 441–448.

12. *Supplement to the Survey of Current Business (BEA-SUP72-01): U.S. Direct Investment Abroad, Part II: Investment Position, Financial and Operating Data* (Washington: U.S. Department of Commerce, 1972), Group 1, table 12, and Group 2, table 12.

13. The dividends and earnings figures are from *Foreign Income and Taxes* (U.S. Internal Revenue Service, Washington, D.C., 1972), pp. 271–273. The interest, royalties, fees, and charges are from the *Supplement to the Survey of Current Business,* cited earlier, Group 1, tables 12 and 23, and Group 2, tables 12 and 23. The Department of Commerce data do not cover quite the same universe as the data of the U.S. Treasury. Moreover, transfer pricing problems affect some of the totals in indeterminate ways. Accordingly, the figures are to be thought of as no more than general orders of magnitude. For the purposes of which they are put in the text, however, the inaccuracies are not critical.

14. This conclusion has required some complex estimating and does not fall readily out of the available data. The raw materials for such estimation are provided in *Foreign Income and Taxes,* cited earlier.

15. See Raymond Vernon, *Sovereignty at Bay* (New York: Basic Books, 1971), particularly chapter 5, "National Economic Consequence." Also R. B. Stobaugh et al., "U.S. Multinational Enterprises and the U.S. Economy," in *The Multinational Corporation: Studies in U.S. Foreign Investment* (Washington: U.S. Department of Commerce, March 1972), vol. 1.

16. For an effort that is more objective than most see J. W. McKie, ed., *Social Responsibilities* (Washington: The Brookings Institution, 1973), forthcoming.

17. Observe that this is the theme of the U.N. Department of Economic and Social Affairs, *Multinational Corporations in World Development* (New York: United Nations, 1973), pp. 75–105.

18. For an elaboration of these problems, see S. M. Robbins and R. B. Stobaugh, *Money in the Multinational Enterprise* (New York: Basic Books, 1973), p. 27, *passim.* See also P. B. Musgrave, "International Tax Base Division and the Multinational Corporation," *Public Finance,* 27, no. 4 (1972), 394–413.

19. The United States has of course already taken such a step in the Revenue Act of 1962, at least with respect to subsidiaries in the developed countries.

20. For an elaboration, see my "Problems and Policies in Competition and Monopoly Power," *American Economic Review, Papers and Proceedings,* May 1974.

21. Note the elaborate provisions on this subject developed in the late 1940s and incorporated in chapter 5 of the aborted Charter for an International Trade Organization.

22. D. H. Blake, "The Internationalization of Industrial Relations," *Journal of International Business Studies,* 3 (Fall 1972), 17–31; also

Karl Casserini, "The Challenge of Multi-National Corporations and Regional Economic Integration to the Trade Unions, Their Structure and Their International Activities," in Hans Gunter, ed., *Transnational Industrial Relations* (London: Macmillan, 1972), pp. 70–93.

23. For statistical purposes, the U.S. government collects extensive data on the offshore activities of its enterprises, but these are only made available in anonymous aggregates, not by individual enterprises.

FIVE

The Foreign Multinational Company in the United States

Arnold W. Sametz

Professor of Finance
New York University

AGENDA AND APOLOGIA

In this wide-range survey of the role of the foreign multinational company in the United States proximate answers have been sought to three basic questions:

1. What are the dimensions of the recent surge of foreign direct investment (FDI) in the United States? What are the facts?

2. Why is the rise of the foreign MNC in the United States occurring now, i.e., since 1966? What are the basic current determinants of FDI in the United States?

3. How does the U.S. subsidiary of a foreign MNC differ operationally from the foreign subsidiary of a U.S. MNC? What are the key operational characteristics of the new entrants into multinational business?

These questions are listed in order of increasing difficulty and the answers are unabashedly of an increasingly tentative nature. The canvas is huge and the brush strokes rough in the interests of providing a useful overall view of the foreign MNC in the United States. This approach also allows a number of broad comparisons to the more familiar role of the U.S. MNC overseas.

Before concluding, we will turn from the foreign investor to raise questions about the United States as a host nation.

Neither the motives nor the operations of foreign subsidiaries in the United States can be assessed from inferences regarding the motives and operations of the U.S. subsidiaries overseas. Indeed, even a priori reasoning suggests that the impacts of FDI and the MNC on a most developed host country are probably quite different from the impacts of U.S. investment on less or lesser developed countries.

In general, it is the inappropriateness of a framework of simple reversibility—i.e., projecting motivational and operational principles that may or may not be applicable to U.S. MNCs overseas to foreign MNCs in the U.S.—that requires us to raise all the basic questions anew. But if we cannot imply foreign direct investment behavior in the United States from U.S. direct investment behavior overseas, our insights into foreign MNCs are sharpened by the contrasts.

Given the range and complexity of the questions raised, the paper has been kept manageable by restricting the sphere of concern to European manufacturing subsidiaries in the United States.

Data and sources for the generalizations of the text are largely confined to footnotes; and no hypothesis, much less a set of hypotheses or a model, is subjected to rigorous testing. But, on the other hand, no hypothesis is unsupported or weakly supported by a handful of "selected" case studies. At the very least, we offer a set of plausible hypotheses whose testing would comprise worthwhile and ambitious research projects. In short, the state of arts in the analysis of the foreign MNCs (in the U.S.) has grown beyond the "for instance" and case study approaches but we are not ready for full-scale model building and testing. But we can, I believe, generalize fruitfully about the distinctive motivations and operational characteristics of U.S. based subsidiaries of European MNCs.

THE DIMENSIONS OF THE RECENT SURGE OF
FDI IN THE UNITED STATES

Although U.S. direct investment in Western Europe ($30.7 billion) in 1972 was triple that of Western Europe in the U.S. ($10.4 billion), Europe's *total* long-term investment in the U.S., i.e., direct plus portfolio investment, exceeded the U.S. totals in Europe by 18 percent ($43.3 billion vs. $36.6 billion). Plainly, it cannot be differences in aggregate wealth, savings or investments that explain the contrasting *composition* of foreign investment. The explanation rather should be sought in investors' choices—the attractiveness of the "broad, deep and resilient" U.S. capital markets to European individuals, and the preferences of European businessmen to export to rather than to produce directly in the United States. And it is to shifts in these preferences that one first turns for explanations of the shifts since 1966 in the composition of European investment in the United States.

Between 1950 and 1972, except for the European preference for foreign equity shares and U.S. preference for direct foreign ownership, the total long-term foreign investment positions were proportionally stable ($3 billion U.S. and $5 billion Europe in 1950 vs. $36 billion and $43 billion in 1972). Today European equity in U.S. industry totals $30 billion of which $20 billion is noncontrolling common stock ownership; the United States has $34 billion of European equities of which $31 billion is in the form of direct investment (see Table 5-1).

In 1950, the two areas had almost identical (cross) direct investment of about $2 billion; over the twenty-two years since then, U.S. direct investment in Europe grew over fifteenfold while Europe's in the United States grew but fivefold. The surge in U.S. investment was particularly heavy between 1959 and 1966, so strong that, for the first time, our total long term investment exceeded Europe's in this country.

However, 1966 was the high water mark. Since that date—and this latter period gets the bulk of our attention—European direct investment in the United States has surged relative to the reverse flow, and

Table 5-1

WESTERN EUROPEAN AND U.S. PRIVATE
FOREIGN INVESTMENT
SELECTED YEARS, 1950–1972
(in billions of dollars)

	Western European Private Investment in the U.S.				U.S. Private Investment In Western Europe			
	1950	1959	1966	1972	1950	1959	1966	1972
Direct Investment	2.0	3.3	6.3	10.4	1.7	5.3	16.2	30.7
Portfolio Investment								
Bonds	0.1	0.4	1.5	8.7	0.1	0.3	0.8	0.3
Stocks	2.0	6.9	8.7	19.5	0.4	1.5	1.6	3.3
Other long-term claims	0.9	1.0	1.3	4.7	0.9	1.1	2.1	2.3
Long Term	5.0	11.6	17.8	43.3	3.1	8.2	20.7	36.6
Short Term	2.8	4.4	9.7	9.0	0.4	0.9	2.6	5.3
	7.8	16.0	27.5	52.3	3.5	9.1	23.3	41.9

Source: "The International Investment Position of the U.S." *Survey of Current Business,* August 1973, table 3, p. 21 and various earlier annual reportings of the Investment Position.

its total investments in the United States resumed its lead, this latter occurring quite apart from the extraordinarily heavy rise in net short-term investments by Europe.

Comparing 1959–1966 and 1966–1972, the rate of growth of U.S. FDI in Europe fell from 17 percent per year to 12 percent while Europe's in the United States rose from 5 percent to 14 percent. Considering just foreign direct *manufacturing* investment, the recent European surge is even more striking: U.S. investment in manufacturing in Europe has grown at a fairly steady 13 percent per year since 1950, while Europe's rate of growth in manufacturing investment in the U.S. leaped to 18 percent per year for 1966–1972 as compared to a steady 6 to 7 percent (half the comparable U.S. rate) for

various prior periods (see Table 5-2). For example, Europe's manufacturing investment in the United States almost doubled between
1966 and 1971 ($2.3 billion to $4.5 billion) while our investment in
Europe increased by under 75 percent ($8.9 billion to $15.5 billion;
see Table 5-3).[1]

Table 5-2

ANNUAL RATES OF GROWTH OF FOREIGN DIRECT
INVESTMENT—THE U.S. IN EUROPE AND EUROPE IN U.S.
1950–1972
(in percentages)

	1950–1959	1959–1966	1966–1972
Total Foreign Direct Investment			
U.S. in Europe	13	17	12
Europe in the U.S.	8	5	14
Foreign Direct Investment in Manufacturing			
U.S. in Europe	13	13	13
Europe in the U.S.	6	7	18

Source: N. Faith, *The Infiltrators* (New York: E. P. Dutton, 1971), table on p. 14,
extended by use of later data from *Survey of Current Business.*

Table 5-3

FOREIGN INVESTMENT IN MANUFACTURING—
THE U.S. IN EUROPE AND EUROPE IN THE U.S.
SELECTED YEARS, 1950–1971
(in billions of dollars of book value)

	1950	1959	1962	1966	1970	1971
Europe in U.S.	0.7	1.5	1.8	2.3	4.1	4.5
U.S. in Europe	0.9	2.9	4.9	8.9	13.7	15.5

Source: "U.S. Direct Investment Abroad, 1971," *Survey of Current Business*, November 1972, table 4, pp. 24–25, and earlier annual reports of this series.

Just as the recent growth in European direct investment in the United States is especially marked for the manufacturing sector, so it is more marked when Europe is sectored: it has been faster for the European Economic Community than all of Europe, and faster for Germany than the whole EEC (see Table 5-4). And European direct investment in the United States has grown faster than the entire world's direct investment in the United States.[2] However, we confine ourselves henceforth largely to European direct manufacturing investment in the United States. Not only is this the focus of the recent shifts in investment trends, but the European share is 70 percent of total FDI in the United States and almost half of Europe's direct investment in the United States is in manufacturing.

Table 5-4

FOREIGN DIRECT INVESTMENT IN THE U.S.
BY AREAS FOR SELECTED YEARS, 1950–1971
(in billions of dollars)

	1950	1962	1971
From Europe	2.2	5.2	10.0
From the EEC	0.7	1.7	3.7
From Germany	0.1	0.15	0.8

Source: "Foreign Direct Investments in the U.S., 1952–1971," *Survey of Current Business,* February 1973, table 1, p. 30, and *Foreign Business Investments in the U.S.,* Department of Commerce, 1962, table 3, p. 36.

To put aside foreign (i.e., largely Dutch and British) ownership of U.S. oil and other raw materials is not at all unusual, for the motivational and operational differences from manufacturing are so great. With greater regret are European (largely UK) direct investment in U.S. *financial* businesses omitted from consideration, for they have been important and probably could be analyzed within a similar framework. Neglected, too, are Canada's and Japan's direct investment in the United States—the former though large is special ("branch-plant" nature) and not surging; the latter, though small, is growing very fast but is likely to be explicable in much the same framework that applies to, say, Germany.

Furthermore, we do not consider the shift of European direct investment overseas from less developed country (LDC) areas to developed areas. We assume that, like the U.S. trends and for similar reasons [3]—both increasing risks of FDI in LDCs and the increasing returns from FDI in developed countries—Europe's direct investment has increasingly been made in relatively developed countries.

Our question is, why, among the developed countries, has the United States become the new focus of Europe's direct investment? Answers to this question should contribute to the broader question —of even greater significance—to what extent, and why, the focus of European foreign investment shifted from the least developed nations to the most developed nation?

WHY THE CURRENT SURGE OF EUROPEAN DIRECT MANUFACTURING INVESTMENT IN THE U.S.?

Understanding the basic motives of U.S. MNCs to own overseas manufacturing capacity in Europe is not of much direct help in understanding the recent reverse flow (i.e., the recent European flow to the U.S.) aside from the similarity of underlying differentiated oligopolistic drives. The MNC is everywhere a predominantly large enterprise operating with economies of scale in mass markets. Traditional European oligopolies (Lever, Pechiney, Siemens, etc.) are little different from their U.S. counterparts. Nevertheless, the precipitating motives that drove U.S. industry to multinationality in the 1950 to 1965 period (especially 1959 to 1965) in Europe are not the same as those driving European industry to multinationality via direct investment in the United States since 1966. And this means that except for the old established European MNCs, application of the U.S. model *in reverse* is not helpful in understanding current investment trends or in estimating cost/benefit impacts on the host countries involved.

To point up the contrast, let us first state the case briefly and crudely:

1. While U.S. direct investment in Europe waited on the development of an adequate size of *market,* European direct investment in the U.S. waited on the development of an adequate size of *company.*

2. European MNCs cannot be said to have located in the U.S. market primarily as a *defensive* measure, to hold markets previously established there via exports, as is said of U.S. subsidiaries in Europe. Truth lies closer to the opposite view: European companies want subsidiaries in the United States as an *offensive* measure; i.e., to strengthen their capacity to compete with the United States in the world and European (home) markets.

3. Although both of the above arguments are dependent in good part on the evolution of the Common Market, and their implementation facilitated by recent changes in the value of the dollar, so, too, were the "size of market" and "defensive" explanations for the surge of U.S. direct investment in Europe.

The EEC is crucial for it provided the arena for the mass intra- and intercountry merger movement that permitted a number of European companies to achieve the giant size that seems prerequisite to success as an MNC; and it provided a "home" market sizeable enough for the profitable application of economies of giant scale. Many of the enlarged European companies have recently established or acquired subsidiaries in the United States to acquire the technology of large-scale production and the techniques of large-scale marketing. The objective is much more to increase the parents' competitive capacity at home (in Europe) than to sustain the parent's role in overseas markets (in the United States). The U.S. MNC, having *begun* the overseas investment game with a large-scale home market and scale technology, was stimulated by the creation of the EEC, which created another mass market which might learn to serve itself if left unchallenged. While from the U.S. point of view it was the size of the European market that changed (via the EEC) and thus stimulated FDI by the United States in Europe, it was the size of the European company, not the size of the U.S. market, that changed (with the EEC) and thus stimulated FDI by Europe in the United States.

The undervaluation of the dollar in 1973 no doubt further stimulated continental direct investment in the United States as it lowered the price of the real American assets (especially via acquisition of undervalued common stocks) and increased the delivered price of U.S. imports. But the surge of European investment in the United States got underway while the dollar was still overvalued, i.e., when European exports to the United States were being stimulated.

We hypothesize that established, internationally oriented firms of Europe prefer to supply their markets in the United States via exports and that the newer overseas investors in the United States are more in search of mass market techniques to bring home.

Again, an exception to this broad generalization must be made for the old, established European giant MNCs—especially in raw materials—which predate the U.S. MNCs. Direct investment by such firms in the United States is probably better explained in terms of countervailing power in the oligopoly power game in the absence of effective international cartels; such investment probably also explains a good part of the cross-direct investment flows. So, too, the older giant MNCs, such as Lever, are exceptions for they are similar to U.S. MNCs in their global marketing of differentiated products. But in terms of the number, if not the value, of additional U.S. affiliates established by European enterprise, such traditional direct investment does not seem to be the heart of the recent and current surge of European direct investment in the United States. Hard data to support these hypotheses are yet to be found or developed; the evidence is indirect and circumstantial.

4. Finally, by contrast to direct investment by U.S. MNCs, neither the host country nor the home country is motivated to handicap the overseas investment. The United States, unlike France, is a most congenial host, for the short-run balance-of-payments gains are not offset by fears of loss of control over strategic sectors or processes. Indeed, U.S. governmental units encourage FDI in the United States. For example, various states, especially in the southeastern region of the United States, subsidize the financing of subsidiaries locating in their regions. The (European) home country has little cause to inhibit their newer MNCs, for the likelihood that their activities are export-displacing is even less likely than for the U.S. MNCs overseas. And to the extent that the financing of the overseas investment is subsidized or arranged by acquisition via exchange of shares or raised by borrowing in the Eurobond markets, there is likely to be a relatively smaller drain on the balance of payments via the financial accounts.

Even if it is not of intimidating size, the U.S. subsidiary in Europe adds to its unpopularity by its tendency to do its basic R & D at home and its continuing financing overseas. European subsidiaries in the U.S. are more likely to be doing their research and development (R & D) in the United States [4] and, as we will see, are more likely to be internally financed, i.e., to restrict dividend flows back to the European parent. In political and sociocultural terms, the EEC is not, or at least not yet, an equivalent set of united states. The role of U.S. plant and equipment overseas is small in relationship to all manufacturing investment in all of Western Europe, but it looms large, say, in the computer industry in France. Foreign companies do not own, nor are likely to own a substantial share of any manufacturing sector in the United States, although they are a very significant factor in pharmaceuticals.

Even the well-known, uniquely American, alleged "obstacles" to FDI in the United States, such as the antitrust laws and the SEC regulations, are in the overall sense offset by uniquely American counterpart "aids," such as the more open and competitive U.S. product and factor markets (in part the consequence of antitrust law enforcement) and broad and deep capital markets (in part the consequence of SEC operations).

Of course, particular cases may turn on food and drug law and immigration restrictions and the like. But in general, uniquely American law would seem to have offsetting advantages for foreign direct investors, or perhaps most often disincentives prove to be of peripheral importance. However, insofar as the "take-over" is of unique importance to European FDI in the United States, the antitrust and SEC authorities are likely to be frequently involved, but this concerns inhibition of a particular *method* of FDI, not FDI itself. Furthermore, insofar as uncertainties about antitrust prosecution is a seriously inhibiting factor, it should be more threatening to the traditional giant European MNC than to the technique-seeking subsidiary that has become so important in the last five years.

In general, the current European surge of direct investment in the United States is primarily a function of home market needs and owes far more to industrial organization theory than to trade theory or investment theory. As Raymond Vernon has pointed out, European technology has traditionally specialized in material- and land-saving as contrasted with U.S. specialization in labor-saving technology.[5] Recent developments in Europe—widened markets and labor shortages—have increased the attractiveness, if not the necessity, of U.S.-type technologies.

The aim seems to be: Learn by doing to become a Big U.S. Company rather than learn by selling in the Big U.S. markets. In either case, it is the *size* of the market rather than its growth rate or the barriers around such markets that is the prime factor in stimulating foreign direct investment.[6] Little success has been reported in relating FDI to profitability. In this case, the lack of correlation perhaps can be attributed to the fact that long-run profit of the whole company or sales maximization is of central concern. This in turn is primarily European market oriented, and the long-run fortunes are presumably furthered by new technological and marketing know-how acquired by the subsidiary in the United States.[7]

The typical new European subsidiary in the United States is more a substitute for factor importing than for commodity exporting; it is more akin historically to investing in raw materials abroad than in productive capacity abroad.[8] The usual product cycle analysis as developed by Professor Vernon would seem then less applicable to European investment in the United States than to U.S. investment in Europe. The U.S. MNC first developed mass production especially for the home market, then for export markets, and then production overseas to hold the new mass-sized European markets. For these companies FDI can be thought of primarily as defensive—to hold on to overseas markets first developed via exports. The European MNC's prime objective in the United States is centered on the first stage—the development of mass-production capacity for the enlarged home market; the product cycle in this sense has not begun.

In other words, European FDI in the United States is primarily concerned with real factor transfers, such as know-how; it finds no substitute in other forms of foreign investment, i.e., portfolio investment in the United States. Nor is foreign trade, i.e., exports, a likely alternative, as is often argued for U.S. FDI in Europe. It is for these reasons that international organization theory rather than investment or trade theory seems even more central to the European MNC activities in the United States than to MNCs of other nationalities.

And it is clear, too, why European MNCs have been concentrating their FDI in the United States in recent years. It is not, as is fashionable to say, that Europeans have gotten over their fears of the American market which they now feel free to invade; rather it is that Europeans are tooling up here to contain or roll back the American invasion of their European markets.[9] True, the confidence of European international corporations that they could hold U.S. export markets may be shaken by the recent successive devaluations of the dollar. But for direct investment purposes, the undervaluation of the dollar can be thought of as having a short-run impact on European exports to the United States; its primary and long term impact is to make it cheaper to acquire U.S. subsidiaries.[10]

European MNCs are also positively inhibited from attempting to produce in the United States for the U.S. market by the large size required for economical entry. The economically required size for a French subsidiary to produce in the mass U.S. market may make that subsidiary larger than the parent! Such a subsidiary would add substantial risk to the whole MNC and would involve disturbing managerial challenges.

The average size of European affiliates is far smaller than those of the United States, expecially newer affiliates. The United States, with 55 percent of the stock of foreign direct investment in the developed countries, had 35 percent of the total number of affiliates; while Germany, for example, with less than 5 percent of the total stock had 11 percent of the number of affiliates.[11]

The shift in Europe's international investment position should be thought of as more from foreign portfolio investment to foreign direct investment than from exports. And as we now will see, European emphasis on acquisition of existing companies as subsidiaries is closer to simple portfolio investment in equities than is the establishment of a subsidiary *de novo,* the more typical route for the U.S. MNC in Europe.

WHAT ARE THE KEY COMPARATIVE OPERATIONAL CHARACTERISTICS OF EUROPEAN SUBSIDIARIES IN THE UNITED STATES?

Given the purposes of recent European FDI in the United States, as contrasted with that of the U.S. MNC activity in Europe, it should not be surprising that subsidiary operational characteristics differ. In a nutshell, recent European subsidiaries—having been established in high technology industries, to carry out R & D activities in the United States and to develop new products rather than to protect old markets—are characterized by substantial independence of parent management, unusual dependence on acquisition or take-over techniques, and heavy use of internal finance as compared to European subsidiaries of U.S. MNCs.

Relatively great *subsidiary independence* is a necessity when the subsidiary is carrying on specialized activities quite different from those in which the parent excels. Parent control is quite different when the subsidiary is simply a sales outlet for products formerly exported. But even here, the subsidiary's necessarily large size (for effectiveness in the American market) would add to its independent stance. The technology-seeking subsidiary is more dependent on the U.S. technology leader than on the European parent. Such a subsidiary is likely to have special managers (including native Americans), to be insulated from the sales and export markets which are the prime concern of the parent, and to be more oriented to doing business with other U.S. companies than with U.S. consumers. All of which is to say that close integration with the parent managers is less necessary and perhaps even would be harmful to the special tasks of the subsidiary.[12] And insofar as antitrust action is feared, subsidiary independence would strengthen the company's defenses.

Similarly the special tasks of the typical new subsidiary—to gain quick and then deep access to U.S. technological and marketing skills —makes the *acquisition* of an appropriate going concern a popular technique. Daniels found that twenty-five out of his sample of forty recently established subsidiaries were established via the acquisition route; the other fifteen tended to be involved with marketing an unique product or a former export.[13] The acquisition route has also been favored in 1972 and 1973 by the combination of undervaluation of the dollar and the undervaluation (low price-earnings ratios) of U.S. equities. But it is inhibited by the antitrust authorities' attitudes toward acquisition versus *de novo* branches or subsidiaries. The principal point must be that acquisition of a subsidiary is the natural method when the prime objective is the acquisition of U.S. business techniques of production and marketing.

Note, too, that it is easier for a European company to acquire a company in the United States when shares are widely owned in deep capital markets than it is at home. While 10 to 15 percent of the value of U.S. direct investment in Europe (1963 to 1968) took the acquisition route, that route perhaps accounted for half of Europe's investment in the United States.[14] In terms of numbers of affiliates, the ratios are about three-fifths for European versus one-quarter to two-fifths for U.S. acquisitions as a percentage of total affiliates established in the 1946 to 1967 period.[15]

Such established units, once acquired, are also likely to be financed primarily via *retained earnings* and depreciation flows for that is, after all, the "native" way, i.e., the predominant means of financing U.S. corporations. Moreover, the overseas unit was wanted to "remit" techniques, not short-run cash dividends to the parent. Besides accounting methods in research-oriented firms do not tend to yield much in the way of reported profits. If the firm's acquisition of the subsidiary was financed by an exchange of shares, the subsidiary will have a large unused capacity to borrow. For the period 1964 to 1971, European manufacturing subsidiaries in the United States retained 58 percent of earnings which met 53 percent of total needs. On the other hand, U.S. manufacturing subsidiaries in Europe retained 42 percent of earnings which met 45 percent of financial needs.[16]

Over the period 1967 to 1971—the period of rapid growth of European FDI in the United States—the expected decline in the significance of internal financing did not take place. Retained earnings for European manufacturing subsidiaries in the United States were 62 percent of total earnings and supplied 55.5 percent of total funds required, as measured by the increase in book value of direct investment.[17] In other words, retention was stepped up more than sufficiently (58 to 62 percent) to meet the previous proportion of total financing needs. Ordinarily, one expects the proportion of financing needs met internally to fall during an investment boom.[18] This all testifies to the unusually heavy financial role of internal finance for U.S. subsidiaries of European MNCs.

In the process of praising "well-behaved" European subsidiaries in the United States, as contrasted with the "ugly Americans" abroad in Europe, Nicholas Faith noted the tendencies of European subsidiaries to be more willing to share equity and management with the natives (i.e., Americans) and to introduce new products.[19] To say that there is no *Défi Européen* is to make a virtue of necessity. In any case, it further supports the case for the basic differences in operation of European subsidiaries in the United States.

CROSS-INVESTMENT PATTERNS AND THEIR WELFARE AND POLICY IMPLICATIONS

The underlying differences in purpose and function between the European MNCs in the United States and the U.S. MNC in Europe, which have been stressed in this paper, suggest that cross-investment patterns are to be expected. Quite apart from the interpenetration of each other's markets by the giant multinational obligopolies, which can be explained in terms of game theory in the absence of overt cartels, simultaneous investment abroad by both U.S. and European MNCs in the same industry, even in the same product line, can be explained in terms of different objectives. These differences —older versus newer European MNCs or U.S. versus European MNCs in general—suggest that the national economic and financial impacts of MNC activities are unlikely to be simple.

In particular, the assumption of simple reversibility of impacts is not likely to be very helpful in drawing out the implications of the recent surge of FDI in the United States by European MNCs. For example, for recent U.S. investment abroad, a leading issue has been the export-displacing effects of that FDI on the balance of payments; it would not be helpful to assume that German investment in the United States is likely to be reciprocally import-displacing. Nor are the domestic employment or domestic investment impacts likely to be similar but reversed. One possible pattern is that U.S. FDI in Europe per dollar is more stimulating to employment, investment, GNP, etc. in the overseas host country than is European FDI in the United States—based on the assumption of the output-orientation of U.S. FDI and the input orientation of European FDI.[20]

The sociopolitical impacts of cross-investment also are not simply reversible. The relative size of the United States and the U.S. MNC and the average size of its FDI (which is of necessity located within a particular nation's boundaries) results in a high proportion of ownership and control of total plant and equipment (Canada), of a whole industry (computers in some countries), or of part of an industry (certain chemicals). Such large shares have no counterpart for European FDI in the United States. Some illustrative figures follow. The U.S. MNC is responsible for 10 percent of gross plant and equipment investment in the EEC and 20 percent in the United Kingdom alone. European MNCs account for less than 1 percent of gross plant and equipment expenditures in the United States. While U.S. corporations own about 5 percent of total corporate assets in Europe, European corporations own about one-quarter of 1 percent of U.S. corporate assets ($10 billion out of $2,500 billion).

However, there are the traditional oligopolistic bases for rational cross-investment: differentiated products are imperfect substitutes, and oligopolistic leadership may be less threatened by expansion overseas.[21] While necessary to remember that there are two quite distinct sets of European MNCs, the traditional MNC—the truly interchangeable giant company—is not the leading edge of the recent rapid growth in European MNCs with which we have been concerned.

Insofar as European direct investment in the United States is defensive or market-oriented like U.S. investment in Europe, there will be simpler cross-investment patterns. There has been an intensification of factors stimulating to such defensive investment in the last few years: the more rapid increases in labor costs in Europe than in the United States, new stress on the aggregate risk-reducing aspects of international diversification, improved financing capacities both via internationalization of capital markets and subsidies by U.S. regional governmental units, a general catching-up in retaliatory capacity of the traditional giant European MNCs, continental exchange rate shifts, and the surge in European company size. But many of these factors are stimulating to all forms of FDI, and defensive investment is not the predominant mode of European FDI in the United States.

The difficulties of measuring costs and benefits of FDI are neither eased nor multiplied by the fact of cross-investment patterns. The assumption of perfect reversibility is unwarranted. But even if it were, the assumption is not of much help so long as the basic cost/benefits accounting of one-way FDI remains primitive.

Even our understanding of cross-investment patterns is slim. Aside from basic industrial organization theory and examples of oligopoly rivalry, we may find current cross investment activities of European MNCs explicable in terms of differences in the stage of the product cycle and of what might be called the exchange-rate cycle. On these grounds, the recent high rate of growth in European FDI in the United States may well be sustained through the 1970s. But such growth does not imply nor require that the rate of growth of U.S. FDI in Europe be correspondingly constrained.

Business groups have found no difficulty in finding arguments (say, employment increasing) to support FDI flows both to and fro. On the other hand, we have learned that trade union hostility to FDI abroad does not mean that trade unions will smile on FDI in the United States.

We are hardly ready to make policy in this area; but it should be acknowledged that the fact that there are different determinants, purposes, and functions of American and European subsidiaries alone assures that argument by simple analogy will not do. On the other hand, the uncovering of these differences does suggest, à la comparative advantage, that flows in both directions may be beneficial to all.[22]

NOTES

1. Note that although the rates of growth have been reversed, the absolute size of the gap is still rising.
2. Continental Europe's share of total FDI in the United States has risen steadily since 1959 from one-third to two-fifths; the rest is largely provided by the United Kingdom (one-third) and Canada (one-fourth).
3. I have concerned myself with "The Decline of Private Foreign Investment in the LDC's—Causes and Cures of the Widening Gap," a study undertaken as part of a larger project on *The Multinational Firm in the U.S. and World Economy*, being conducted at New York University's Graduate School of Business Administration. (New York: Salomon Brothers Center for the Study of Financial Institutions, Working Paper no. 2, April 1973).
4. "Roughly 70 percent of the European Companies with U.S. opera-

tions in our sample reported that they do R & D in the U.S.," from Lawrence G. Franko, *European Business Strategies in the U.S.* (Geneva: Business International, 1971), p. 23.

5. *Sovereignty at Bay* (New York: Basic Books, 1971), pp. 79–81 and 109–11. U.S. concern with environmental externalities may well lead to U.S. "import" of European materials-savings techniques.

6. See the model and references to Scaperlanda's and Mauer's work in *The Survey of Current Business,* February 1973, pp. 35 and 39–40.

7. It should be noted that profitability of a specific subsidiary of an MNC is unusually difficult to estimate owing to the effects of variable transfer prices and taxes on reported profits and the differential discounts for risk. And in any case, it is the addition to total MNC profits that is central. Recognizing the "portfolio" aspect of a MNC's package of overseas subsidiaries also complicates interpretation of reported profits data; the domestic countercyclical attribute of a foreign investment will via diversification increase the quality (reduce the risk discount) of its expected profitability. It has been noted, too, that profit rates are more likely to be correlated by industry than by country.

8. European FDI has always been more heavily involved with the LDCs than U.S. FDI principally because of their relative emphasis on the search for raw materials rather than markets for developed country products, except "low-end," e.g., textile products. For example, 38 percent of UK and 45 percent of French FDI is in LDCs as compared to 28 percent for the United States (*Multinational Corporations in World Development* [New York: United Nations, 1973], table 12, p. 148).

9. Even with a fully achieved EEC, competitiveness will probably be less intense than in the U.S. market, while the still larger U.S. market will probably continue to be technologically more rewarding, at least for the next decade.

10. True, the older established MNCs in the U.S., primarily those of Canada and the United Kingdom, are more export-oriented; but theirs are not the currencies that have been sharply revalued vis-à-vis the dollar.

11. *Multinational Corporations in World Development* (New York: United Nations, 1973), tables 4 and 5, pp. 138–139.

12. See Franko, *op. cit.,* chapter 4, pp. 35 ff. See also J. N. Behrman, *Some Patterns in the Rise of the Multinational Enterprise* (Chapel Hill: University of North Carolina, 1969), pp. 100–103; and J. S. Arpan, *International Intracorporate Pricing* (New York: Praeger, 1972), pp. 67–68.

13. See J. D. Daniels, *Recent Foreign Direct Manufacturing Investment in the U.S.* (New York: Praeger, 1971), p. 62.
14. See Rainer Hellman, *The Challenge to U.S. Dominance of the International Corporation* (New York: Dunellen, 1970), p. 257; and S. E. Rolfe and Walter Damm, *The Multinational Corporation in the World Economy* (New York: Praeger, 1970), p. 81.
15. *Multinational Corporations in World Development,* table 36, p. 186. And Franko (*op. cit.,* p. 49) writes: "European corporations seem to have a preference for acquisitions as opposed to formulation of U.S. subsidiaries."
16. Calculated from table 5, pp. 36–37 of the *Survey of Current Business,* February 1973, and table 4, pp. 24–25, *ibid.,* November 1972.
17. *Ibid.*
18. The sharp rise (from 45 to 52 percent) in the ratio of internal financing to total new investment of U.S. manufacturing subsidiaries in Europe (1967 to 1971) was the expected consequence of declining growth rates and a decline in the *needs* for external funds. The proportion of total earnings retained rose only from 42 percent to 44 percent.
19. Nicholas Faith, *The Infiltrators* (New York: E. P. Dutton, 1972), p. 5.
20. From the standpoint of *world* welfare, such a set of effects of cross-foreign direct investment would be ideal in that it tends to equalize per capita output in the developed world while easing the U.S. balance-of-payments problem.
21. Almost half of U.S. FDI is undertaken by industries in which the top four firms account for at least 75 percent of output. It has been estimated that two-thirds of all U.S. FDI in Europe is attributable to twenty firms. See Christopher Tugendhat, *The Multinationals* (New York: Random House, 1972), p. 30; and Behrman, *op. cit.,* pp. 43 ff.
22. But to what degree is this evaluation dependent on assumptions of competitiveness or, at least, that similarly motivated oligopolistic cross-flows are not dominant? To repeat: we are hardly ready to make policy in this area.

Bibliography

Arpan, Jeffrey S. "Made in the U.S. by Foreigners." *Atlanta Business Review*, September 1972.

——— *International Intracorporate Pricing*. New York: Praeger, 1972.

Behrman, Jack N. *Some Patterns in the Rise of the Multinational Enterprise*. Chapel Hill: University of North Carolina Press, 1969.

Caves, Richard E. "International Corporations: The Industrial Economics of Foreign Investment." *Economica*, February 1971, pp. 1–27.

Damm, Walter "The Economic Aspects of European Direct Investment in the U.S." In S. E. Rolfe & Walter Damm, *The Multinational Corporation in the World Economy*. New York: Praeger, 1970, pp. 35–51 and Appendix A.

Daniels, John D. "Recent Foreign Direct Manufacturing Investment in the U.S." *Journal of International Business Studies*, Summer 1970, pp. 125–132.

——— *Recent Foreign Direct Manufacturing Investment in the U.S.* New York: Praeger, 1971.

Dunning, John H. *Studies in International Investments*. London: Allen & Unwin, 1970.

Ekblom, H. E. "European Direct Investments in the U.S." *Harvard Business Review*, July/August, 1973, pp. 16–27.

Faith, Nicholas *The Infiltrators*. New York: E. P. Dutton, 1972.

Franko, Lawrence G. *European Business Strategies in the U.S.* Geneva: Business International, 1971.

Hellman, Rainer. *The Challenge to U.S. Dominance of the International Corporation*. (New York: Dunellen, 1970), chapters 6 and 9.

Katz, Stanley S. "Foreign Direct Investment in the U.S." In *U.S. International Economic Policy in an Interdependent World.* Washington, D.C.: Report to the President by the [Williams] Commission on International Trade and Investment Policy, 1971, pp. 965–980.

Multinational Corporations in World Development. New York: United Nations, 1973.

Richardson, David J. "Theoretical Considerations, in the Analysis of Foreign Direct Investment." *Western Economic Journal,* April 1971, pp. 87–98.

Roback, Stefan "The Silent Invasion." *World Magazine,* January 16, 1973, pp. 26 ff.

Survey of Current Business:
  "Foreign Direct Investment in the U.S., 1962–1971," February 1973.
  "Foreign Direct Investment in the U.S. in 1972," August 1973.
  "The International Investment Position of the U.S. in 1971," October 1972.
  "U.S. Direct Investment Abroad in 1971," November 1972.

Tugendhat, Christopher *The Multinationals.* New York: Random House, 1972, chapters 3–4.

United States Department of Commerce:
  Foreign Business Investment in the U.S., 1962.
  List of Foreign Firms with Some Interest Control in American Manufacturing and Petroleum Companies, February 1972.

Vernon, Raymond *Sovereignty at Bay.* New York: Basic Books, 1971, chapters 3 and 7.

Ward, James J. "Product and Promotion Adaptation by European Firms in the U.S." *Journal of International Business Studies,* Spring 1973, pp. 79–86.